DIVING DEEP

EXPERIENCING JESUS THROUGH
SPIRITUAL DISCIPLINES

LEADER GUIDE

AMY SIMPSON

Group

Loveland, Colorado

Diving Deep Leader Guide
Experiencing Jesus Through Spiritual Disciplines
Copyright © 2002 Amy Simpson

Visit our Web site: **www.grouppublishing.com**

Credits
Editor: Kelli B. Trujillo
Creative Development Editor: Dave Thornton
Chief Creative Officer: Joani Schultz
Copy Editor: Lyndsay E. Bierce
Art Directors: Sharon Anderson, Julia Ryan
Cover Art Director: Jeff A. Storm
Cover Designer: Julia Ryan
Computer Graphic Artist: Joyce Douglas
Cover Photographer: Blanca Middlebrook
Production Manager: Dodie Tipton

ISBN 0-7644-2342-8

10 9 8 7 6 5 4 3 2   11 10 09 08 07 06 05 04 03 02
Printed in the United States of America.

CONTENTS

p**4**   Foreword by John Ortberg

p**6**   Introduction

p**8**   Lesson 1:   Pursuing Jesus
    AN OVERVIEW OF SPIRITUAL DISCIPLINE

p**12**   Lesson 2:   Proclaiming Truth
    WORSHIP

p**18**   Lesson 3:   Me, Myself, and God
    SOLITUDE

p**23**   Lesson 4:   Made for Each Other
    FELLOWSHIP

p**29**   Lesson 5:   The Ugly Truth
    CONFESSION

p**33**   Lesson 6:   Bread of Life
    FASTING

p**37**   Lesson 7:   The Greatest
    SERVICE

p**43**   Lesson 8:   Let's Talk
    PRAYER

p**48**   Lesson 9:   What Really Matters
    SACRIFICE

p**52**   Lesson 10: The More Truth You Know...
    STUDY

p**57**   Lesson 11: Trying to Laugh
    CELEBRATION

p**61**   Lesson 12: Frustration–Free
    SUBMISSION

p**66**   Lesson 13: Turning It Off
    SILENCE

p**72**   Spiritual Disciplines Retreat Plan

p**95**   Scripture Index

Diving Deep: Experiencing Jesus Through Spiritual Disciplines

Spiritual Disciplines

FOREWORD

by John Ortberg

As a general rule at the church where I work, we don't use the word *discipline* a whole lot. It has unfortunately taken on a lot of baggage for most people. They associate it with that which is unpleasant, unfair, or severe.

If this is true for people by and large, it is especially true for young adults who are itching for freedom. Being disciplined generally sounds like being grounded. (Although I, myself, have never been quite clear on exactly what it means to be "grounded." When our kids were five or so, we used to tell them they were grounded from their senior prom.)

Ironically, of course, the whole point of practicing disciplines is to experience freedom. It's the discipline of playing scales that eventually produces a musician who is free to make music, the discipline of running laps that creates an athlete who is free to finish strong in the fourth quarter. The purpose of the disciplines is always freedom.

And this does not cease to be true when it comes to one's spiritual life. When we think of "disciplined people," we generally think of those who engage in many disciplines. But of course, that's not the point. As Dallas Willard has noted, the disciplined person is the one who is able to do the right thing in the right way at the right time. The disciplined basketball player is the one who is able to make the right pass at the critical juncture; the disciplined runner is the one who is able to kick into the homestretch.

And the disciple of Jesus—the "disciplined follower"—is not primarily someone who practices *lots* of spiritual disciplines. It's someone who is able to do the kind of thing Jesus would do in his or her place. It is someone who is able to speak a word of confrontation or encouragement or guidance when it will be most helpful. (And to be silent when that is needed as well!) The purpose of engaging in these disciplines is never to demonstrate how "spiritual" one is. It is not to earn Brownie points with God. It's not a way of separating the deeply committed students from the superficial ones. Spiritual disciplines are a means to an end; and the end that they help us grow toward is simply life: life as Jesus himself lived it, and the life he taught us that we could live as well.

That's why I'm so grateful that Group Publishing has put together this resource. Even more than that, I'm grateful that *you* have picked it up and are considering making the investment of building this material into the lives of the young people with whom you work.

I'm the father of two teenagers, and in a few months our third and final offspring will be in that category as well. When I was in their stage of life, the only two arrows I knew about in the spiritual-growth quiver were prayer and Bible study. As long as I was engaged in something we would call a "quiet time," I felt that my spiritual life was on track. When I wavered, I felt guilty. But there were two problems with this understanding. First, I didn't understand the connection between these spiritual practices and the overall life I was living. I had a vague sense that once my quiet time was done, I could pretty much cross my spiritual obligations off the list for the day. I didn't realize that God wasn't interested in something called my "spiritual life"; he was just interested in my life.

Second, I didn't realize that the training process for spiritual life involves far more than just those two spiritual practices. I didn't understand why solitude could help free me from the need to gain approval from the people around me or how confession could enable me to experience deeper levels of love and greater freedom from sin.

So by embarking on this journey, you are part of a learning process that can help a generation of young people enter into rivers of spiritual nurture that might otherwise take them decades to discover. In a day when it can be tempting for churches to either despair over student ministries or simply try to jam them full of kids by doing whatever activities they think might entertain them or retain their attention, you are seeking to help students enter into a deeper life with Christ. It matters immensely that you do that. Let me offer a few encouraging words as you set off.

Remember that this is not the sort of thing you can teach about from a neutral perspective. Ultimately, the life you reproduce in the students you work with will be the life you live yourself. That means that the practices you teach your students about will be practices you need to engage in yourself. The good news here is that you will discover these to be pathways to a richer life with God for your own soul. Far from simply passing information on to listeners, you will be experiencing life change on your own.

Also, remember that this kind of learning involves experience, not simply head knowledge, and that means you will have to move forward largely by trial and error. When your students (or you, for that matter) begin to practice solitude, for instance, it may be quite a challenge. I remember the first time I set a day apart to be alone with God. I had a list of things to pray about, and I finished it in the first hour or so. Then I just sat there with God. I wished one or the other of us was more talkative! Eventually, I was able to learn wonderful things that day. But I had to learn by trying how it is actually possible to both speak and listen to God. For a generation of young people trained by MTV to have the attention span of a type-A fruit fly, learning to be still and silent will require lots of trial and error. Especially error.

Remember, too, that each one of the young people you work with is unique. Everyone has particular ways in which he or she is most sensitive to respond to God: For some people nature is especially important; some take more naturally to solitude and prayer; others gravitate toward fellowship and relationship. Furthermore, everybody wrestles with particular patterns of sin that make specific disciplines more or less crucial to him or her. People who struggle with sins of appetite or impulse control, for instance, may especially benefit from fasting. Those who are prone to image management may have a stronger need for confession. Which disciplines are most helpful to which people depends on the unique configuration of spiritual strengths and weaknesses that we all carry around with us.

Finally, remember that this is not a group self-improvement process. Its effectiveness does not finally hinge on the students' spiritual prowess, on your giftedness as a leader, or even on the adequacy of the material in this leader guide. It depends on God.

God is at work. The spiritual disciplines are simply a way we open up space for his power in our lives.

And God *will* work. He is always faithful. He wants your students to have the best "grounding" of all—to be grounded in the faith and love that will sustain them throughout their lives.

So enough talking, it's time to get grounded!

John Ortberg is a teaching pastor at Willow Creek Community Church in South Barrington, Illinois. He is the author of several books, including *The Life You've Always Wanted: Spiritual Disciplines for Ordinary People.*

INTRODUCTION

Spiritual disciplines...hmmm. What exactly are we talking about here? Is this some zany new youth ministry strategy, the latest fad sweeping across the country?

Not at all. In fact, spiritual disciplines are as old as Christianity itself. Spiritual disciplines are simply opportunities for Christians to work out their spiritual muscles through exercises such as prayer, fasting, worship, and service. The practice of spiritual disciplines helps us get to know God better. And they're very relevant to your students' lives.

In their book *Millennials Rising*, Neil Howe and William Strauss describe religious trends among the current generation of young people, whom they've dubbed "Millennials": "Millennials think and talk more about faith, and do more with it, than older people realize. It matters to them. In one poll, teens cited religion as the second-strongest influence in  their lives, just behind parents, but ahead of teachers, boy/girlfriends, peers, and the media." Howe and Strauss also claim that today's teenagers are drawn to ancient rituals more than informal contemporary services.

So what does that mean for you? Well, the downside is that teenagers are interested in religion of all kinds. They're exposed to a variety of belief systems, and they're more likely than ever to choose a buffet-style approach to faith, embracing the more palatable aspects of various religions and combining them into their own homespun religions.

On the bright side, teenagers are open to the gospel. And they're hungry for a call to discipleship—especially when that call is wrapped in time-tested biblical practices. According to George Barna, two out of three teenagers strongly desire a personal relationship with God. Wendy Murray Zoba points out that mission trips among teenagers are more popular than ever. According to Christine J. Gardner, "Christian teens are fasting in record numbers. As with their parents, they are searching for a more disciplined spiritual life, but they seem to be more eager to sacrifice pizza for prayer than are older Christians." Today's young people want to be challenged to spiritual growth.

Diving Deep: Experiencing Jesus Through Spiritual Disciplines issues that challenge. This book focuses on twelve different spiritual disciplines and outlines a plan for introducing your young people to each one. Each lesson includes an introduction to the discipline, a study of the biblical basis for that discipline, and an opportunity for teenagers to get a taste of what it means to practice that discipline. This book also includes a retreat plan, designed to be used after the lessons, to help each of your teenagers focus intensively on one particular discipline.

The *Diving Deep Student Journal* will help make this experience more meaningful and lasting for your students. Encourage them to use the journal to record their prayers, thoughts, and  questions during their personal times with God throughout the week. Prompt them to read the biographical pictures of the various disciplines and to use the journaling ideas to enhance their own experiences with this course. Also, make sure each of your students has a journal before using these lessons. They'll use their journals during some of the lessons and during the retreat. (You might even want to use a journal yourself!)

Diving Deep will introduce your teenagers to life-changing practices that can bring them into close contact with God. These lessons are full of powerful experiences that will deepen their faith and inspire them to live in gratitude to God. And they just might change your life too!

AN OVERVIEW OF SPIRITUAL DISCIPLINE—DIVING IN

In *Invitation to Presence*, Wendy Miller writes, "Spiritual disciplines assist us to slow down, to hear, to pay attention, and then to listen for the word of God as it moves from our head into our heart. Once we understand on a heart level, we realize our need to turn to God to receive healing."

Teenagers' lives are hectic and full of the urgent. In the chaos of daily business, it's easy to squeeze God out of their lives. Spiritual growth comes to a halt, and truth goes backstage as the shouting voices of society move to front and center. Teenagers feel their distance from God but don't know how to foster closeness.

Through practicing spiritual disciplines, teenagers can know God better. Disciplines can help students build faith by welcoming God's transforming presence into their lives. This section serves to introduce your students to the importance and benefits of diving into spiritual discipline.

Supplies:

You'll need masking tape, paper, markers, various symbols of athletic training (such as barbells, athletic shoes, a jump rope, hand weights, an exercise mat, a workout video, an aerobic step, a basketball, and an oar), Bibles, *Diving Deep Student Journals*, and pens or pencils.

OPENER

Set out masking tape and a stack of paper. Give each person a marker.

Say: I'd like you to consider some goals for your life. Think about goals you have for the next week, the next year, the next five years, and the next ten years. For example, goals might be "play professional basketball," "become a professional ballet dancer," "make friends in my new neighborhood," "take a dream vacation next summer," "be accepted into the college I want to attend," or "get to know Jesus better."

I'd like you to think of at least one one-week goal, one one-year goal, one five-year goal, and one ten-year goal. Describe each goal on a piece of paper, then tape each piece of paper to any wall in our meeting area.

After each person has had a chance to write several goals, gather everyone back together.

Say Having goals is great and important. But goals don't mean anything unless we take steps to reach them. Let's talk more about what it takes to reach goals.

UNDERSTANDING SPIRITUAL DISCIPLINE

Walk around the room, and stop at several of the papers students hung on the walls. At each one, ask teenagers to call out ways a person might accomplish that goal. List those ideas on the paper.

After you've listed ways to accomplish several goals, say: **Each of these goals requires discipline to accomplish. You named some disciplines that would help a person achieve those goals, such as practice and hard work. Discipline is also required for us to achieve our spiritual goals, such as knowing Jesus better or being more loving.**

Ask students to form groups of three to five. Give each group a stack of paper, markers, and tape.

Say In your group, compile a list of spiritual goals, or ways people might want to be more spiritually mature. For example, you might say, "love God more," "have stronger faith," "experience joy," "be more loving," or "grow to understand who God is." Write each spiritual goal on a piece of paper, and tape your papers on the walls.

When groups have written and hung up several goals, ask:
- **How do people come up with spiritual goals?**
- **What kinds of things might people do to reach their spiritual goals?**
- **How might setting and reaching spiritual goals change a person's life?**

- **How do you think God feels about spiritual goals?**

Say Two goals that shouldn't be on our list are to earn God's love or make God love us more. We can't earn his favor, and we can't earn our way into heaven. We must accept God's grace and forgiveness. But as a response to that grace and forgiveness, we can set goals to love God more and grow closer to him. Let's look at what the Bible says about this.

SCRIPTURE SOURCE

Ask students to pass around symbols of athletic training, such as barbells, athletic shoes, a jump rope, hand weights, an exercise mat, a workout video, an aerobic step, a basketball, and an oar.

As students pass the objects, ask:
- **What do these objects symbolize?**
- **What result does ongoing athletic activity have in a person's life?**
- **How do athletes use these to reach their athletic goals?**

Say Let's discover something Paul said about spiritual discipline.

As teenagers continue passing around the objects, read 1 Corinthians 9:24-27 aloud. Then ask students to follow along in their Bibles as you read it again.

Then ask:
- **What was Paul talking about?**
- **What did he mean when he said, "Run in such a way as to get the prize"?**
- **Have you ever experienced this type of athletic commitment and discipline? What was it like?**
- **What does this level of discipline look like in other hobbies, such as music or acting?**
- **Why do you think Paul wrote about strict athletic training?**

- **What was he saying about spiritual growth?**

Say? Paul used athletic training to describe the discipline of spiritual growth. Just as physical training builds our strength and health over time, spiritual disciplines build our spiritual strength and health as they bring us closer to Jesus. Let's consider how spiritual disciplines might help us grow.

CONSIDERING DISCIPLINE

Give each person a *Diving Deep Student Journal*. Tell students that these journals will help them document their experiences with the spiritual disciplines. They'll also use the journals throughout these experiences. Encourage them to read the stories and use the journal ideas during their personal time with God throughout the week.

Direct students to turn to page 4 in their student journals and look at the list of spiritual disciplines and their definitions.

Say? Read through this list of spiritual disciplines. Then look at the spiritual goals you and your group named and hung up earlier. Walk around the room, and write under each of your group's goals at least one discipline that might help people reach that goal.

After several minutes, call everyone together and ask:

- **How easy or difficult is it to see connections between disciplines and goals?**
- **What kinds of connections did you find?**

- **Why set spiritual goals?**
- **Why practice spiritual disciplines?**
- **How might spiritual disciplines affect your relationship with God?**

Say? Let's begin to consider how you might incorporate spiritual discipline into your life.

CLOSING

Make sure everyone has a student journal. Give each person a piece of paper and a pen or pencil. Instruct students to write down at least one spiritual goal. Then have students write down in their journals and on the paper you gave them one or two spiritual disciplines they might be interested in practicing in order to reach their goals. When they've finished, collect the papers.

Say? It's great to have this written in your journal to remind you of what you have in mind at this point. Over the next several weeks, we'll be studying each of these spiritual disciplines in detail. As we do, I'd like you to consider focusing on one spiritual discipline and incorporating it into your life for a time to help you grow closer to God.

Close in prayer, asking God to provide your group with wisdom and insight into how spiritual disciplines might build their faith.

Keep the papers you collected from students. Use them to pray specifically for your students and to help them discover the spiritual disciplines that best suit them.

LEADER TIP

As students leave, remind them to take time this week to read

about the desert fathers in their student journals (p. 6)

and record their thoughts and prayers throughout the week.

Try these ideas to incorporate spiritual discipline into your youth ministry program on a regular basis.

• Use the retreat plan in this book (pp. 72-94) to help students further understand spiritual discipline, experience discipline in more depth, and choose what disciplines they might focus on. Repeat the retreat periodically to give students the opportunity to commit to practicing new disciplines in their lives.

[BONUS IDEAS

• Form discipline-accountability pairs. Have teenagers team up with others who want to focus on the same disciplines and then set up plans for holding each other accountable to the practice they commit to.

• Occasionally set aside time in regular youth meetings for students to practice spiritual disciplines or share how such practice is affecting their relationships with Jesus.

• Use the pictures of specific disciplines in this book to teach teenagers about historical or contemporary Christians who have exhibited spiritual discipline. You may want to work together to do further study on some of those people.

• Encourage your students to lead the rest of the congregation in practicing disciplines, either during worship services or in special events or emphases. Your church will be inspired and encouraged to see teenagers' faith expressed in this way.

AN OVERVIEW OF SPIRITUAL DISCIPLINE

PROCLAIMING TRUTH

SCRIPTURE: PSALM 103

WORSHIP

In *The Call*, Os Guinness says, "For some people the grand passion is art, music, or literature; for others the dream of freedom and justice; for yet others the love of a man or a woman. But search as you will, there is no higher or more ultimate passion than a human being ablaze with a desire for God."

Teenagers are passionate people. Adolescence is a time of strong emotions and roller-coaster mood swings. In such a tumultuous time, young people need something to believe in and to invest in with their passion.

Through practicing the spiritual discipline of worship, teenagers can experience a deeper appreciation of their relationship with God. Worship builds faith by reminding people who God is and what he does.

OPENER

Before this lesson, write identity indicators on self-stick name tags. You'll need one name tag (and identity) for each person. Here are some ideas for identities you might use:
- homeless person
- professional athlete
- banker
- lawyer
- prom queen
- criminal
- high school teacher
- movie star
- garbage collector
- missionary
- politician

- music star
- millionaire
- drug dealer
- artist

As teenagers arrive, stick a name tag on each person's back. Don't let students see the name tags you're sticking to them. When everyone has arrived, encourage people to mingle.

Say? **Walk around the room, and look at the tags on people's backs. After you see someone's tag, you'll know how to treat that person. Treat that person as if he or she really is the kind of person described on the name tag. As you interact with people, pay attention to how they treat you and the kinds of things they say to you. Try to guess your identity.**

Allow teenagers to spend several minutes mingling. Then call them back together and ask them to guess their identities. Then ask:

- **How did you decide how to treat other people?**
- **How did you try to guess your identity?**
- **What makes us decide how to treat people in real life?**

Say? **The ways we chose to treat one another in this activity weren't always positive. In fact, we probably treated others in some ways we should never treat them in real life, no matter who they are. But this experience makes an important point about today's topic. We should treat God according to who he is and what he does. That's what it means to worship God. Today we're going to talk about how worship can build our faith.**

UNDERSTANDING THE DISCIPLINE

Before this lesson, write out the following questions on a piece of newsprint or a dry-erase board. Display the questions where everyone can see them.

- **Who is in your family?**
- **What are the ages and names of all the people in your family?**
- **What does each person in your family do most of the time?**
- **What three words would you use to describe each person in your family?**
- **If someone made a movie about your family, what would be the title, and why?**
- **What do you like best about your family?**
- **How has your family made you the person you are?**

Have teenagers form pairs.

Say? **Let's explore a little more what it means to worship God. To illustrate what it means, let's spend a little time talking about our families.**

Instruct pairs to spend several minutes discussing the questions you wrote out and displayed earlier. When they've finished, ask each person to share with the group his or her answer to one of the questions. Then ask:

- **How does talking about your family affect your understanding of them?**
- **How does talking about your family affect the way you feel about them?**
- **How does talking about your family affect your understanding of yourself?**
- **How might talking about God affect our understanding of him?**
- **How might talking about God affect our understanding of ourselves?**

Say? **In a way, this exercise was similar to worship. Worship is proclaiming the truth, either to ourselves or to others, about who God is and what God does. Proclaiming this truth can draw us closer to God because it helps us understand and appreciate him more. Worship also reminds us who we are in relationship to God. When we think of worship, we usually think of singing. But there are *many* ways to worship God.**

Ask:

- **What are some different ways we can proclaim the truth about who God is and what God does?**

As teenagers call out ideas, list the ideas on a piece of newsprint or a dry-erase board. If they need ideas to get started, offer these suggestions: praying, telling faith stories, giving money or other resources, and serving others.

Say? These activities all can be ways to worship God. They affirm God's place and our place in the universe. They remind us of who God is and the wonderful things God does. Worship draws us closer to God because it breaks into everyday life and renews our perspective.

SCRIPTURE SOURCE

Be sure each person has a Bible.

Say? Psalm 103 is a great example of one way to worship God. David, once king of Israel, wrote this and many other psalms of praise to God. Psalms were poems set to music, and they've been used in Christian worship for centuries. David used the psalms to proclaim truth about who God is and what God does. Let's read Psalm 103 together in a worshipful way.

Have students form six groups (a group can be one person). Assign each group one of the following Scripture passages: Psalm 103:1-5; Psalm 103:6-8; Psalm 103:9-12; Psalm 103:13-14; Psalm 103:15-18; and Psalm 103:19-22.

Instruct each group to practice reading its assigned verses a few times. Then lead students in reading their parts in order so that they read the entire psalm aloud. If necessary, remind students to read in a worshipful celebratory way to proclaim truth about God.

Then ask:

- **What does this psalm say about who God is?**
- **What does this psalm say about who we are?**
- **What does this psalm say about our relationship to God?**
- **How do you feel about God after proclaiming truth this way?**
- **How do you feel about yourself after this experience?**
- **How can worship help us grow closer to God?**

Say? Worship—proclaiming the truth about God—helps us grow in our faith because it's such a powerful reminder of our place and God's place in the universe. When we remember who God is and what God has done, how can we not respond? God deserves our worship, and worship helps us want to know and serve God more.

PUTTING IT INTO PRACTICE

Say? To practice the discipline of worship, we're going to hold our own worship services.

Have teenagers form groups of three to five people. Point students to the list of ways to worship that the group compiled earlier. If you can, assign each group to a different area of the building so that groups won't be tempted to perform for one another.

Say? I'd like you to hold a worship service within your group. Each person should look at the list of ways to worship and pick one way to worship God. Once you've chosen your mode of worship, either do that worship for your group or lead your group in doing it together. For example, you might want to tell your group a story about how God has worked in your life. Or you might want to lead your group in singing a praise song. Remember that you're worshipping God. Proclaim truth about who God is and what God does. It doesn't matter how well you think you're performing. Worship is not a performance for others!

After groups have completed their worship experiences, ask:

- **What was this experience like?**
- **How did this experience affect the way you feel about God? yourself? others?**
- **How might frequent experiences of heartfelt worship affect your faith? the way you live?**
- **How does worship draw people closer to God?**

Say: **Now let's consider how we might incorporate the discipline of worship into our lives.**

CLOSING

Before this lesson, make a photocopy of the "Weekly Schedule" handout (p. 17) for each person.

Say: **The discipline of worship doesn't have to be something we do only on Sunday mornings. Like other spiritual disciplines, worship should be** incorporated into your daily life. Let's spend a few moments considering how we can do that.

Give each person a photocopy of the "Weekly Schedule" handout. Have students fill in the handout with typical weekly schedules.

When teenagers have finished filling in their schedules, have them go through their schedules and designate ways they can worship God in the midst of those everyday activities, including setting aside times just for focused worship. If they need ideas, refer them to the list of ways to worship God compiled earlier.

Ask each person to share at least one idea from the handout.

Say: **Even if you don't choose to focus on the spiritual discipline of worship, I encourage you to use these ideas to weave worship into your daily life. As you remember who God is and what God does, worship can build your faith and transform your life.**

Close in prayer, asking God to inspire your students to worship in their everyday lives.

LEADER TIP

As students leave, remind them to take time this week to read about Third Day in their student journals (p. 10) and record their thoughts and prayers throughout the week.

Try these ideas to incorporate authentic worship into your youth ministry program on a regular basis.

● Use a variety of worship modes and styles. Put as much thought into the worship portions of your meetings as into the teaching times. Be creative when planning worship, and use as many resources as you can get your hands on. For example, check out Group Publishing's *Worship Ideas for Youth Ministry* or *Worshipmania*.

● Give teenagers a chance to focus on worship. So often, we spend so much time teaching young people about God that we neglect time spent in response to God. Occasionally forego the talk or lesson, the games, and the announcements and just worship!

● During times designated for worship, think twice about the silly songs and hodgepodge of selections. Choose songs and activities that proclaim truth about who God is and what God does. Creatively pick selections that support a common theme.

● Keep worship fresh and surprising by using various props and settings. For example, you could hold a worship service at the zoo and focus on God's creativity. Look through encyclopedias for specific things to praise God for.

● Especially during times of worship, remind teenagers often of the purpose of worship. Reinforce the idea that worship is proclaiming truth about who God is and what God does. It's not about performing for others or merely socializing.

WEEKLY SCHEDULE

	Sunday	Monday	Tuesday	Wednesday	Thursday	Friday	Saturday
7							
8							
9							
10							
11							
12							
1							
2							
3							
4							
5							
6							
7							
8							
9							
10							

ME, MYSELF, AND GOD

SCRIPTURE: MARK 1:35-39; 6:45-51; 14:32-43

SOLITUDE

In his classic *Celebration of Discipline*, Richard Foster writes, "Solitude is more a state of mind and heart than it is a place. There is a solitude of the heart that can be maintained at all times. Crowds, or the lack of them, have little to do with this inward attentiveness. It is quite possible to be a desert hermit and never experience solitude. If we possess inward solitude we do not fear being alone, for we know that we are not alone. Neither do we fear being with others, for they do not control us...Whether alone or among people, we always carry with us a portable sanctuary of the heart."

Don't you wish that kind of peace and inner strength for yourself? for your teenagers? Rather than peace, most people carry around with them enormous burdens. Yet the busyness and distraction of our whirlwind society keep us from recognizing and unloading those burdens.

Through practicing the spiritual discipline of solitude, teenagers can reconnect with God one-on-one. Solitude builds faith by forcing us to depend on God for relationship and for the truth about life.

Supplies:

You'll need a dry-erase board or newsprint, a marker, pens, *Diving Deep Student Journals*, photocopies of the "Strength in Solitude" handout (p. 22), scissors, Bibles, photocopies of the "Time Alone With God" handout (p. 22), and blank invitations.

OPENER

Display a dry-erase board or a piece of newsprint where everyone can see it. Divide it into two columns. When everyone has arrived, direct teenagers' attention to the columns you've created. Then ask:

● **How did you prepare for your day today?**

As teenagers call out ways they prepared for their day, list everything they name in the left-hand column. Encourage students to list *everything*: dressing, brushing their teeth, planning their day, eating breakfast, and so on.

When you've compiled a list of preparations, ask:

- How would you have prepared if you were going to spend the entire day alone—you wouldn't see a single person?

   As teenagers call out ideas, list them in the right-hand column. Then ask:

- What kind of differences do we see between our two lists?
- Why do you think those differences appear?
- Why do other people affect the way we live?
- How can other people affect the way we experience God?

Say: Relationships are great, and we all need other people in our lives. In fact, through relationships we often experience what God is like. But we also need time alone, away from other people and the relationships that influence us. Other people can distract us from focusing on God. That's why the spiritual discipline of solitude—or being alone—can be helpful to spiritual growth. Let's learn more about the discipline of solitude.

UNDERSTANDING THE DISCIPLINE

Say: I'm going to send everyone out in a different direction. The point is for each person to spend some time alone. Even if you can see other people, completely ignore everyone else. Just focus on what you experience. Take notes in your journal on everything you observe. Be sure to tune in to all your senses.

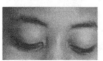 Give each person a pen, and make sure each person has a student journal. Send everyone out in a different direction, either outside or in the building. If necessary, stagger groups a minute or so apart, a few kids at a time, so that they're on their own.

   After five to ten minutes, gather everyone back together.

   Ask:

- What kinds of things did you notice?
- How would this experience have been different if you'd been with someone else?
- How did it feel to be alone?
- How were those feelings different from what you might have felt if you had been in a group?
- How does being alone affect us in real life?
- How might times of solitude build our faith in God?

Say: Solitude takes us away from the distractions and distortions of being with others. In a crowd, we're influenced by the voices and actions of others. We start to believe things that aren't true about ourselves and the world. We forget about some of the things that are important in life. When we spend time in solitude, we can reconnect with God one-on-one, and we tend to gain a fresh perspective on life. And as we depend on God for relationship, we grow closer to him.

SCRIPTURE SOURCE

   Before this lesson, make one photocopy of the "Strength in Solitude" handout (p. 22) for each person. Cut off the "Time Alone With God" section from the bottom half of each copy.

Say: There is a great example for us in the Bible of someone who practiced solitude: Jesus. Jesus often spent time by himself praying. Let's dig deeper into Jesus' model for us.

   Have teenagers form three groups. Assign each group one of these Scripture passages: Mark 1:35-39; 6:45-51; and 14:32-43. Give each person a copy of the "Strength in Solitude" handout and a pen.

Say: In your group, look up the Scripture I assigned you. Then go through the handout I gave you and discuss the questions listed. Write your answers on the handout.

When groups have finished working, have a reporter from each group share the group's answers. Then ask:

- **Why do you think the Bible bothers to tell us that Jesus spent time in solitude?**
- **How does Jesus' time in solitude seem to have affected his ministry?**
- **How might times of solitude affect our ability to minister to others?**
- **How can solitude build our faith?**

Say Being alone with God can be a powerful experience. It can give us fresh perspective on what's important in life. And it can bring us strength to face life's challenges. Let's practice a brief time of solitude now.

PUTTING IT INTO PRACTICE

Give each person a copy of the "Time Alone With God" handout, a Bible, and a pen.

Say We're going to spend fifteen minutes in solitude. The handout I've given you will help guide your thoughts as you spend time alone with God. Because we aren't used to this sort of thing, this activity may be uncomfortable, and fifteen minutes may seem like a long time. But I encourage you to stick it out and see what you can accomplish during this time. You don't have to be still or even silent during this time. I suggest you pray, listen to God, ask God to guide your thoughts, move around, talk aloud, or even sing quietly. Just don't disturb others or pay attention to anyone else. Take advantage of this time to be  with God one-on-one. You may want to close your eyes if that will help keep you from being distracted by others.

Instruct each person to find a place to be alone. Use the entire building if possible, or as much of it as is available. Instruct students to return

in fifteen minutes. During the time of solitude, you may want to walk around the building or the area to make sure teenagers aren't distracting one another.

After fifteen minutes, gather everyone back together. Then ask:

- **What did you think of this experience?**
- **What made this experience easy or difficult for you?**
- **How did this time of solitude affect you?**
- **How might regular times of solitude be faith-building experiences?**

Say It is possible to incorporate the spiritual discipline of solitude into your life. It's easy to get away by yourself, even for just five minutes a day, and that time of solitude with God can have a big impact in your life.

CLOSING

Give each person a blank invitation and a pen.

Say Even if you don't choose to focus on the spiritual discipline of solitude, it's a great idea to spend time alone with God. God is inviting you to spend time with him, away from the distractions and distortions of human life. Consider this an invitation from God. I'd like you to think about how God might write that invitation and fill it in as if God had written it to you. Think about where and when God might want you to spend time alone with him. Would it be in your bedroom in the morning? in a church near your school in the middle of the day? in a closet in your house? in the park or at the beach after school? Remember, it doesn't have to be a quiet place or even a comfortable place, just a place where you can be alone with God. Think of a place and time that would work, and fill out your invitation.

Give teenagers a few minutes to create their invitations. Then ask:

- **What are some ideas you came up with?**

Allow volunteers to share their ideas. Then close in prayer, asking God to tug at the hearts of everyone present and inviting everyone to spend time alone with God.

Encourage teenagers to take their invitations home and use them as reminders to spend time alone with God.

LEADER TIP

As students leave, remind them to take time this week to read about Michelle Tumes in their student journals (p. 14) and record their thoughts and prayers throughout the week.

Try these ideas to incorporate solitude into your youth ministry program on a regular basis.

[BONUS IDEAS

• Every now and then, forego the large-group meeting. Instead, encourage teenagers to spend time in solitude (during your usual meeting time), considering a topic or a set of questions you give them beforehand. The next time you meet, ask them to share with the group what they learned during their time of solitude.

• Provide your church as a place where teenagers can find solitude. Set aside a prayer room that people can sign up for, or make a room available during certain hours.

• Plan a special "retreat of solitude" for your students. Have participants gather on a Saturday and go to a park or some other inspiring place. Ask everyone to bring Bibles, blankets, song books, and journals. At the park, each person can find a place to be alone with God for two hours. Have everyone gather at the end for worship and debriefing.

STRENGTH IN SOLITUDE

Read your assigned Scripture passage, and discuss the questions below with your group. When necessary, explore the verses before and after your Scripture passage to discover the answers to the questions.

What happened before Jesus went into solitude? ....

....

How do you think Jesus felt before he went into solitude? ....

....

Why do you think Jesus decided to spend this time alone? ....

....

What happened after Jesus spent this time in solitude? ....

....

How did Jesus' time alone seem to have affected him? ....

....

TIME ALONE WITH GOD

As you spend time in solitude, use this as a guide to make your time valuable.
Tune out all distractions. Ignore other people. Concentrate on being alone. Pay attention to your thoughts and feelings.

- **Consider what's important in life. What really matters? How do you spend most of your time and energy? How *should* you spend most of your time and energy? What needs to change in your life?**

- **Consider your relationship with God. What's good about that relationship? What about that relationship is not healthy? What's missing? What are you thankful for?**

- **Read a favorite Scripture passage. What does God want to say to you through this Scripture?**

- **Don't think about others—just be alone with God.**

MADE FOR EACH OTHER

SCRIPTURE: EPHESIANS 4:11-16

FELLOWSHIP

According to Charles Swindoll in *Rise & Shine*, "The church was never meant to be merely a set of buildings where you come, sit, worship, learn, and leave. The church is a community of believers who demonstrate genuine concern for each other." Swindoll goes on to say, "Fellowship occurs, I believe, when there are *expressions of genuine Christianity freely shared among God's family members*."

Our society is characterized by hunger for community. And teenagers, like the rest of us, crave connections. They're surrounded by people most of the time—at school, at the mall, at sporting events, at home. But presence doesn't mean connection. In fact, surface encounters can leave teenagers feeling lonely and empty.

Through practicing the spiritual discipline of fellowship, teenagers can experience God through one another. Fellowship builds faith by giving us a reminder, a representation, of what God is like.

Supplies:

You'll need a TV, a VCR, the movie *It's a Wonderful Life*, photocopies of the "Fellowship Gifts" handout (p. 28), scissors, envelopes, gift bows, snacks, Bibles, a gift-wrapped box, a toy boat, a baby doll, a (G-rated) anatomy book or poster, poster board, markers, and tape or tacks.

OPENER

Before the lesson, set up a TV and VCR in your meeting area. Cue up a tape of the movie *It's a Wonderful Life* to the scene toward the end of the movie when the angel, Clarence, shows George Bailey what life would have been like if George had never been born. Set up the tape to start right after George and Clarence are thrown out of Nick's bar. If you set your VCR counter to 0:00.0 when the studio logo appears at the beginning of the film, this clip begins at approximately 1:50:45.

To begin the lesson, introduce the movie clip.

Say: **We're going to begin the lesson today by watching a clip from the classic movie *It's a Wonderful Life*. In this movie, George Bailey has reached the end of his rope. He feels like a failure, as if his life has meant nothing. In fact, he contemplates ending his life because he believes he's worth more dead than alive. He wishes he had never been born.**

LEADER TIP

Well, God sends an angel named Clarence to help George Bailey. Clarence wants to show George that his life has been significant, so he tells George he has gotten his wish: He was never born. George ventures out into the town to discover that life is very different from the way he thought it was. He sees his hometown and the people in it as if he had never been born and had never made an impact on their lives. Let's see what that looks like.

Show the clip from *It's a Wonderful Life*. Stop the tape at approximately 1:58:20 when George looks at the camera in terror and then Clarence says, "Every man's life touches so many other lives." (This clip lasts approximately seven and a half minutes.)

Say: **This movie clip shows the importance of each person's contributions, even the small things.**

Ask:

• **What do you think George Bailey learned from this experience?**

• **What does this illustrate about the lives of people?**

• **Why do people sometimes feel as if their lives are insignificant?**

• **How does being connected to other people affect our lives?**

Say: **Today we're going to talk about intentionally being connected with other people through the discipline of fellowship.**

UNDERSTANDING THE DISCIPLINE

Before the lesson, make at least one photocopy of the "Fellowship Gifts" handout (p. 28), and cut apart the slips. You'll need enough slips for each person to have one. Put each slip inside its own envelope, and put a gift bow on each envelope. If you're really ambitious, put each slip of paper inside a box, and gift-wrap the boxes. Also set out some snacks for students to eat during this activity.

Say: **Fellowship is the discipline of being with**

others in ways that help us grow in our faith. It's more than just hanging out with other people. Fellowship encourages people, reminds them who God is, and builds their faith.

Give each person one of the gift envelopes with a slip of paper inside. Have students open their envelopes.

Say Inside your envelope is a specific kind of gift you can give someone else through fellowship. During the next five minutes, give that gift to as many people in this room as possible.

After five minutes, call everyone together and ask:

- **What was this experience like?**
- **What is fellowship like in real life?**
- **What are some other ways to have fellowship with one another?**
- **How can fellowship help us grow in our faith?**
- **How can we avoid taking fellowship for granted?**

Say Let's consider some things the Bible says about fellowship.

SCRIPTURE SOURCE

Make sure each person has a Bible. Read Ephesians 4:11-16 aloud while students follow along.

Have teenagers form four groups. Assign each group one of the images in the text: God's gifts, infants, ships, and the body of Christ. Give 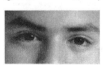 each group an object to represent its image: group one should have a gift-wrapped box, group two a toy boat, group three a baby doll, and group four a (G-rated) anatomy book or poster. (You can find anatomy charts in most encyclopedias.)

Say As a group, study the passage and discuss the image I've assigned you. Decide what the image represents and what Paul was trying to say

through that image. When you've finished discussing, you'll explain the meaning of your image to the rest of us, using the symbol I gave you. Focus specifically on what that image says about the importance of fellowship.

Allow groups a few minutes for discussion, then ask each group to present the meaning of its image and how that image relates to fellowship. When groups have finished their presentations, ask:

- **Why did God give us different gifts?**
- **What does that say about the importance of fellowship?**
- **What do the other images say about how fellowship can help build our faith?**
- **Why do you think God created us to need one another?**
- **Why might some people need to practice fellowship as a discipline?**

Say Fellowship may seem like an obvious, natural part of our lives. But remember, fellowship is a special kind of being together.

PUTTING IT INTO PRACTICE

Say Fellowship with others is a gift. By encouraging one another, sharing our lives, being honest, forgiving, and reaching out, we give gifts to other people. These gifts start with God. He gives all of us gifts and expects us to use them to build our faith and the faith of others. Some of us need to spend more time with other Christians. Others need to make that time count. Even though we may be spending plenty of time with other Christians, we need to purposely make that time fellowship by sharing our gifts.

Instruct each person to think of a gift he or she can share with someone else to help that person experience and remember God's truth. Then ask each person to share that gift with at least one other person in the room.

Allow a few minutes for students to share their gifts of fellowship, then ask:

- How do you feel about this experience?
- How is fellowship different from just being together?
- How might our group be different if all our time together was spent in fellowship?
- How can this kind of thing help people understand God better?

Say: There's a reason God created us to need one another. We experience God through fellowship.

CLOSING

Encourage teenagers to get comfortable and close their eyes.

Say: Picture a campfire. It has been burning for a while, and you're sitting next to it at night, staying warm. The logs are turning white, and the flame is low. The embers glow red with heat. They feed on one another, keeping the fire going.
Every now and then, a spark flies out from the fire and lands on the ground. It glows for a few seconds, then grows cold and dies out.
You pick up a stick and spread apart the coals. You feel a blast of warmth as the trapped heat is released into the air. Then the air begins to grow colder. The fire is slowly dying as the embers struggle to burn on their own. You watch as the glowing turns to sputtering and finally to cold, dead ashes.

Encourage students to open their eyes.

Say: We're responsible for keeping the fire going in one another's lives.

If we don't have fellowship with one another, our faith will grow colder or die out. We experience God through fellowship with one another. Fellowship can help us stay strong in our commitment to Christ.

Give each person a poster board. Set out markers where everyone can use them.

Say: Create a poster. On one portion of your poster, list gifts you can give others to make your interactions true fellowship and to help others grow in their faith.

Give teenagers a few minutes to write.

Say: Now make another list. This should be a list of what you need from other people—gifts others can give you to help you grow in your faith.

When students have finished with their posters, close in prayer, asking the Holy Spirit to be present in your group and to help you experience true fellowship with one another.

Hang the posters in your meeting area.

Say: Even if you don't choose to concentrate on fellowship as a spiritual discipline, I encourage you to consider incorporating these ideas into your life. When we're together as a group, these posters can help us remember to give one another the gift of true fellowship.

LEADER TIP

As students leave, remind them to take time this week to read about the early church in their student journals (p. 18) and record their thoughts and prayers throughout the week.

Try these ideas to incorporate fellowship into your youth ministry program on a regular basis.

• Use a spiritual gifts inventory and your own observations to help teenagers discover their own spiritual gifts. Then help them come up with specific ways to use those spiritual gifts to encourage one another. You may even want to form teams of people to exercise specific spiritual gifts in fellowship with one another.

[BONUS IDEAS

• Have fun! Give teenagers plenty of opportunities to practice being the body of Christ by just having fun together. Be a community.

• Create a team of adults and teenagers responsible for building and maintaining fun, friendly, Christ-like fellowship.

• Instead of automatically discouraging talking, recognize that some teenagers may sometimes need fellowship more than a time of worship or teaching. Ask teenagers who need to talk to do so in a specific area of the room, where they won't disturb others. Station an adult in that area to make sure fellowship is positive and productive.

• Set up a space that encourages fellowship: Use inviting colors, comfortable furniture, some tables, friendly decorations, and warm lighting.

• Be bold about confronting teenagers who resist fellowship. If necessary, help them with strategies to experience successful fellowship. They may avoid reaching out to others because they don't know how.

FELLOWSHIP GIFTS

Photocopy this page, and cut apart the slips of paper below.

Listen attentively to someone.

SHARE A STORY FROM YOUR OWN LIFE WITH SOMEONE.

Share a snack with someone and chat.

Remind someone about a specific characteristic of God.

TELL A FUNNY AND APPROPRIATE JOKE TO SOMEONE.

Remind someone about a funny or meaningful memory of a past experience with that person.

Compliment someone.

PRAY WITH SOMEONE.

Tell someone about your family.

Ask someone about his or her future plans.

WORK TOGETHER WITH SOMEONE TO TIDY UP THE ROOM.

THE UGLY TRUTH

SCRIPTURE: JAMES 5:13-16; 1 JOHN 1:8-10

CONFESSION

In *Too Busy Not to Pray*, Bill Hybels said this about confession: "This approach to confession, unfortunately, is a colossal cop-out. When I lump all my sins together and confess them en masse, it's not too painful or embarrassing. But if I take those sins out of the pile one by one and call them by name, it's a whole new ball game."

Confession isn't popular among teenagers or anyone else. In a world of excuses and pointing fingers, we're reluctant to admit we've done wrong, let alone that we deserve punishment. Without confession, we remain closed off to the acceptance of forgiveness.

Through practicing the spiritual discipline of confession, teenagers can see their own sin-stained state in contrast to God's perfection. Confession builds faith by making us aware of our desperate need for God's forgiveness and the magnitude of that gift.

Supplies:

You'll need newsprint or a dry-erase board; a marker; Bibles; and one piece of fruit that can be peeled—such as bananas, oranges, or grapefruit—for each person.

OPENER

When everyone has arrived, write this saying on a piece of newsprint or a dry-erase board where everyone can see it: "Confession is good for the soul."

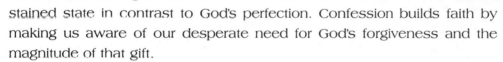

Ask:
- **What does this saying mean?**
- **What is confession?**
- **Why and how might confession be good for a person's soul?**

Say: **Confession is telling the truth about what we've done and admitting our**

responsibility. Let's consider how confessing our sin—the wrong things we do—can help us grow in our faith.

UNDERSTANDING THE DISCIPLINE

Have students form pairs.

Say: Tell your partner a story about something you got in trouble for when you were a child. Be sure to tell the naked truth—no holding back or trying to make yourself look good.

Ask:
- What was it like to tell your partner about getting in trouble?
- Were you tempted to put a positive spin on the story or rationalize it to make it sound not so bad? Explain.
- In real life, how do we rationalize or put a spin on the truth of our actions?
- What's the purpose of confession?
- How does confession affect our relationship with God?
- How do we confess our sins in real life?

Say: The purpose of confession is to help us experience true forgiveness. If we try to hide our sin or pretend it's no big deal, we don't truly feel our need for forgiveness. But if we confess our sin to God and others, we're forced to face the ugly truth about our desperation before God. We see ourselves in contrast to God's perfection. Then when we experience God's forgiveness, we realize how incredible it is and how much we have to be grateful for. As others forgive and accept us, we see tangible symbols of God's grace. Let's take a look at what the Bible says about confession.

SCRIPTURE SOURCE

Make sure each person has a Bible. Ask a volunteer to read aloud James 5:13-16 while everyone else follows along. Then ask:
- According to this Scripture passage, to whom should we confess?
- What is the result of denying or trying to hide our sin?
- What is the result of confession?

Ask another volunteer to read aloud 1 John 1:8-10. Then ask:
- According to this Scripture passage, to whom should we confess?
- What is the result of denying or trying to hide our sin?
- What is the result of confession?
- Why is confession so valuable?
- How might confession bring us closer to Christ?

Say: God wants us to confess our sins, not because confession is good for God but because it's good for us. It helps us truly experience God's amazing grace and forgiveness. Let's practice the discipline of confession now.

PUTTING IT INTO PRACTICE

Before the lesson, arrange for a caring, gracious, trusted adult to be available for students who need to spend extended time in confession during this activity.

Say: This is an opportunity for us to confess our sin to God and other people. It's a bold step in our culture to confess to someone else, and that step is not required here. However, I encourage you to try confessing sin to me or someone else here who you trust.

Encourage each person to find his or her own private space in the room, as far away from others as possible.

Say: Let's spend a few minutes in confession. You can confess your sin to God silently or aloud. You can go to someone else and confess your sin to that person. If someone confesses to you, listen with love and grace. Remind that person of God's forgiveness, and rely on God's help to forgive the person yourself. Remember, the benefit in this comes in your honesty.

Allow a few minutes for students to confess to God and one another. Then quietly call everyone back together. If some students begin to dig deep into some serious issues and need more time for personal confession, allow those students to remain in one area of the room and continue the exercise. Ask the adult you recruited beforehand to tend to those students, comforting them and assuring them of God's forgiveness.

CLOSING

Say: God has forgiven you! Whatever you just confessed to God has been wiped away. God looks at you as if you had never done those things.

Give each person a piece of fruit that can be peeled, such as a banana, an orange, or a grapefruit.

Say: I'm going to lead you in an object lesson, and I'd like you to do it along with me. Then we'll go straight into our closing prayer.

Begin to peel a piece of fruit, and continue peeling as you talk.

Say: This piece of fruit represents your life. You're covered in the peeling of image. We all want to be seen as better than we are; we all want to believe we're better than we are. But God knows our sin, our shortcomings, and our needs. In order for us to truly experience God's forgiveness and acceptance, we must become aware of our sin, our shortcomings, and our needs. We must strip away our excuses, masks, rationalization, and denial. Present yourself as raw, exposed, and vulnerable to God and people you trust. Always be aware of your need for forgiveness.

Hold the peeled fruit in your hand and pray aloud: **Dear God, Help us admit to the truth about ourselves, which is...**

Stop and prompt teenagers to fill in the blank silently. Then continue:

Thank you for your forgiveness and the joy that comes in admitting the truth about ourselves and then experiencing your complete forgiveness. In Jesus' name, amen.

LEADER TIP

As students leave, remind them to take time this week to read about King David in their student journals (p. 22) and record their thoughts and prayers throughout the week.

Try these ideas to incorporate confession into your youth ministry program on a regular basis.

• Encourage teenagers to confess their sins to you as a way of experiencing forgiveness. Emphasize that they need to confess to God as well but that confessing to you can help them face the truth about themselves. When teenagers do confess to you, be sure to respond to them not with shock or condemnation but with grace, love, and forgiveness. Reflect Christ!

[BONUS IDEAS

• Frequently provide opportunities for teenagers to stop what they're doing (during activities or worship) and confess to one another the ways they've wronged one another. Emphasize the need for them to truly forgive one another and start with clean slates in their relationships.

• Teach frequently about God's grace and forgiveness. This topic should be the theme of your teaching just as often as issues of behavior, morality, or anything else.

• Always hold a time of confession before your group participates together in the Lord's Supper.

• Create a "confession bank." Make a box, tub, or other container with a slot on top. Keep a supply of small papers and pens nearby. Encourage teenagers to write notes of confession and put them in the bank as a tangible way to confess their sins to God. Be sure no one but you ever has access to the confession bank.

FASTING

In his book *Walking With Saints*, Calvin Miller talks about predators that steal peace from our lives. The first one he mentions is "our culture of convenience." He describes the way this culture steals peace from our lives:

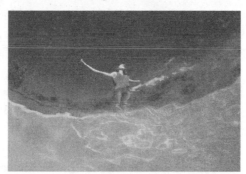

"We are deceived into believing that material abundance grants us peace, not that it steals it. But steal it does. For no matter what life gives us, we always want more. Our craving for things never sleeps long enough to allow us peace. We are the walking wanton."

Teenagers have been trained to search for fulfillment in material goods, personal comfort, pleasure, and escape from reality. Like most of us, they travel a path of constant consumption, always seeking the next greater source of happiness, and they never find the fulfillment they're looking for.

Through practicing the spiritual discipline of fasting, teenagers can experience fulfillment in their relationships with God. Fasting builds faith by removing distractions and forcing people to become dependent on God.

OPENER

Before the lesson, set out a TV, and turn it on or play a video. Set out popcorn or other fragrant snacks, a computer (turned on), books, a CD player and CD (turned on), mail-order catalogs (with a variety of merchandise), and sale fliers from a variety of stores.

When everyone has arrived, say: **As we begin our lesson, let's just focus on God.** Pause for a few minutes. Then turn off the stimuli in the room.

Supplies:

You'll need a TV, a VCR and video (optional), popcorn or other fragrant snacks, a computer (optional), books, a CD player and a CD, mail-order catalogs (with a variety of merchandise), sale fliers from a variety of stores, newsprint, a marker, tape or tacks, a dry-erase board and two colors of markers or a chalkboard and two colors of chalk, paper, an eraser, Bibles, one slice of bread for each person, index cards, and pens.

Ask:

- **What was it like to try to focus on God during this time?**
- **What made it challenging for you to focus on God?**
- **What real-life distractions did these symbols in our meeting area represent?**
- **What other real-life things can keep us from focusing on God?**

As students call out ideas, make a list of them on a piece of newsprint. Then hang the list on the wall for use later.

Say: **Today we're going to talk about fasting, a spiritual discipline that seems out of place in our fast-paced, consumer-driven culture.**

UNDERSTANDING THE DISCIPLINE

Say: **When people talk about fasting, they're generally talking about denying oneself food for a period of time. But we can fast from other things besides food. Our lives are full of distractions. Many of those distractions aren't bad in themselves, but they can keep us from depending on God. We can fast from any of those distractions in order to grow closer to God.**

Ask:

- **What are some needs we all have?**

As students call out ideas, write them on a dry-erase board or a chalkboard. If students need help getting started, you may want to suggest needs such as food, shelter, love, and friends.

Say: **We all have real needs, and that's OK. But God wants us to depend on him to meet our needs. Instead we often try to meet those needs through the distractions in our lives.**

In a different color of marker or chalk, draw a line through each need you listed on the dry-

erase board or chalkboard.

Say: **Maybe we try to deny that the needs are there by watching TV or listening to music.**

In a third color of marker or chalk, circle each need you listed.

Say: **Maybe we try to make our needs look better by buying things.**

Cover the list of needs with paper.

Say: **Maybe we try to cover up our needs with food or relationships.**

Remove the paper.

Say: **No matter what we do, our needs are still there. But when we fast, we say "no" to distractions, and we're forced to face the needs we have. Then when we turn to Jesus with our needs, he can fill our lives and wipe out our needs.**

Erase the list of needs. Ask:

- **Why do we try to meet our needs through what's around us?**
- **Why don't the distractions of life satisfy our needs?**
- **How does fasting help us turn to God?**
- **How can fasting build our faith?**

Say: **Let's look further into how Jesus meets our needs.**

SCRIPTURE SOURCE

Make sure each person has a Bible. Read aloud John 6:35 while students follow along.

Ask:

- **What was Jesus saying in this verse?**

Give each person one slice of bread. Have students form groups of three or four. Then have each group come up with at least three ways Jesus is like bread in our lives. As they come up with their ideas, have students eat their bread as a symbol of Jesus' presence in their lives.

Then ask:

- **How is Jesus like bread?**
- **How does Jesus meet our needs?**
- **How do we try to meet our needs in other ways?**
- **How might our faith grow when we say "no" to those other ways of meeting needs?**

 Say? **We all have important needs, and we sometimes turn to the world around us to try to meet those needs. Saying "no" to certain things in our lives can remind us to let Jesus meet our needs.**

PUTTING IT INTO PRACTICE

Say? **Since this discipline involves saying "no" to something for a certain period of time, we can't truly practice fasting right now. However, we can talk about how we might do it.**

Have teenagers form pairs.

Say? **Look at the symbols I assembled in this room. Also read through the list we compiled in our opening activity. Decide on one thing that keeps you from focusing and depending on God. Then outline for your partner a fasting plan: Talk about how long you think you might fast from that distraction and how you would say "no" to it. For**

example, perhaps you could fast from the television for an entire week, or you could fast from eating lunch once a week or once a month.

Allow a few minutes for partners to talk. Then ask volunteers to share their plans.

Ask:

- **If you were to follow through on this plan, how might it affect your daily life?**
- **How might this fast affect your relationship with God?**
- **How does fasting build a person's faith?**

Say? **Let's consider specifically how Christ can meet your needs as you consider fasting.**

CLOSING

Give each person an index card and a pen.

Say? **We read and discussed John 6:35 earlier. Remember the metaphor Jesus used: "I am the bread of life." Think about what you might fast from in your life. I'd like you to come up with a new metaphor to describe how Jesus can meet your need in that fast. For example, if you're considering fasting from music for a few days, you might write, "Jesus is the music of my life."**

Give students a few minutes to create their metaphors. Then ask volunteers to share what they created, along with the specific ways they're thinking of fasting.

Say? **Take your card with you. If you decide to carry out your fast, put the card in your pocket as a reminder to turn to Christ to meet your needs.**

Close in prayer, thanking Jesus for being the bread of life and for meeting our needs.

LEADER TIP

As students leave, remind them to take time this week to read about Richard Foster in their student journals (p. 26) and record their thoughts and prayers throughout the week.

Try these ideas to incorporate fasting into your youth ministry program on a regular basis.

[BONUS IDEAS

• Hold a one-day fasting retreat. Each person should pick something to fast from. Minimize distractions, and provide ways for people to express what they're experiencing with God, such as times of worship, discussion of how God meets our needs, and journaling exercises.

• When teenagers come to you and express needs in their lives, encourage them to fast in specific ways that will make those needs more real and help them turn to God. Process with them what they experience and learn.

THE GREATEST

SCRIPTURE: MARK 9:33-35; JOHN 13:1-15

SERVICE

In *Ragman and Other Cries of Faith*, Walter Wangerin, Jr. writes, "You say: 'But how can I serve the Lord? I'm not important. What I do is so common and of little consequence. Anyone can do what I do.'

"But I say to you: 'Every time you meet another human being you have the opportunity. It's a chance at holiness.' "

Most of us, including teenagers, value the idea of serving others. But it's easy to "serve" with the motive of receiving something in return. True service requires us to give humbly without expecting anything for ourselves.

Through practicing the spiritual discipline of service, teenagers can become humble before God; their human pride and arrogance are stripped away. Service builds faith by bringing us to the humble position in which we recognize our need for God's grace.

Supplies:
You'll need photocopies of the "Service Projects" handout (p. 42); scissors; Bibles; pens; paper; supplies as necessary to complete service project in "Putting It Into Practice" section (p. 39); newsprint or dry-erase board; a marker; small hand towels, pieces of cloth, or rags; and permanent markers or fabric markers.

OPENER

Say: Let's begin this lesson with a short quiz. Think about your answers to these multiple-choice questions.

Ask:
- **What would you do if you showed up as a guest at a banquet and found out that all the food servers had gone on strike?**
  a. Leave—no food, no fun.

b. Pound your silverware on the table until someone brings you some food.

c. Strap on an apron and start carrying food.

● What would you do if you were shopping in a department store and an elderly woman, who obviously thought you worked there, asked you where to find the shoe department?

a. Say, "I don't work here," and walk away.

b. Yell, "Could someone *please* help this woman so I can get on with my life?"

c. Offer to push the woman's cart as you lead her to the shoe department.

● What would you do if you were at your little brother's band concert and a teacher mistook you for one of the fifth-graders and told you to get to work setting up chairs?

a. Pretend you didn't hear the teacher.

b. File a lawsuit for character assassination and emotional suffering.

c. Flex your muscles, move some chairs, and show everyone what fifth-graders are made of.

Say? Well, as you may have guessed, this lesson addresses the spiritual discipline of service. Let's explore what that is.

UNDERSTANDING THE DISCIPLINE

Before the lesson, make at least one photocopy of the "Service Projects" handout (p. 42), and cut apart the slips of paper. You'll need one slip of paper for each person.

Say? To better understand service, let's go ahead and serve each other.

Give each person a slip of paper from the "Service Projects" handout.

Say? I'd like you to follow the instructions on your slip of paper.

Allow a couple minutes for people to complete their service projects, then ask:

● What was this experience like for you?

● Were some of you surprised that you had to serve but no one served you?

● How did it feel to serve and not be served in return?

● How did it feel to be served and not have to serve anyone else?

Say? Those of you who served but got nothing in return experienced true service. Service is like going to a restaurant and paying your money without getting your food. Service requires giving of ourselves and expecting nothing in return. Service puts us in a position of humility, where others aren't impressed with us and may not even notice us at all. There's little human glory in true service.

Ask:

● How might service affect the way others see us?

● How might service affect the way we see ourselves?

● How could service help build our relationships with God?

Say? Let's take a look at what God's Word has to say about service.

SCRIPTURE SOURCE

Make sure each person has a Bible. Read Mark 9:33-35 aloud while students follow along. Then ask:

● Why were the disciples embarrassed when Jesus asked them what they had been talking about?

● According to Jesus, what is the chief characteristic of someone who is great in God's kingdom?

● Why do you think God requires his followers to be servants?

Say: Now let's take a look at another passage about servanthood. But first let me give you a bit of background information. This passage describes something that happened when Jesus and his disciples got together to share a meal shortly before Jesus was killed. In the culture of Jesus' time on earth, people traveled by foot, and they wore sandals. Their feet got very dirty. When people arrived at someone's house, one of the household servants would wash the feet of the people so they could be comfortable. This was considered a very lowly job.

Have students read John 13:1-15 aloud, with each person reading a verse at a time.

Say: Call out words that describe Jesus' position in this group.

If students need help thinking of words, get them started with "God," "teacher," and "master."

Say: Now call out words that describe the household servant who would have washed the feet of the people in this group.

If students need help thinking of words, get them started with "powerless," "lowly," and "outsider."

Ask:

- **What are some of the contrasts between Jesus and the servant?**
- **Why do you think Jesus chose to put himself in the servant's role?**
- **Why do you think Peter was so shocked by what Jesus was doing?**

Have teenagers form groups of two to four. Give each group a pen and paper. Instruct each group to write a story describing a situation like the one described in John 13:1-15. Their stories, however, should have different characters and  settings. For example, a story might describe the owner of a hotel cleaning guest rooms or a king working in a farmer's field.

After a few minutes, ask groups to read their stories aloud for one another.

Ask:

- **What do these stories illustrate about Jesus' example for us?**
- **How can we follow Jesus' example in real life?**

Say: Let's follow Jesus' example right now.

PUTTING IT INTO PRACTICE

Before the lesson, you may want to brainstorm some ideas for service projects that students can choose from in this activity.

Say: Let's come up with a service project that we can do right now. Remember, this project should be one that requires us to give to others without expecting glory or recognition or anything else in return. In fact, this project should help us humble ourselves before God so that our pride and arrogance are stripped away and we're ready to accept God's grace.

Work with the group to develop a service project that really puts them in a humble position, preferably something that will gain them no glory or recognition. For example, they could clean the toilets at the church, clean the toys in the nursery, water the plants in the church, clean the windows at the pastor's house or someone else's house, do landscaping or maintenance on church grounds, or pick up trash in a park.

Then join students in completing the project, taking as much time as you can. After the project, ask:

- **What was difficult about this project?**
- **What was rewarding about this project?**
- **How is this kind of experience faith-building?**

Say: Let's consider how we can incorporate this kind of service into our everyday lives.

CLOSING

Say: Earlier we studied Jesus' example of service and considered the significance of his washing the disciples' feet. In the church, people sometimes wash one another's feet as a way of following Jesus' example. Knowing what we know about the significance of that act in Jesus' day, let's consider what we could do for others that puts us in the kind of humble position Jesus was in.

Have students consider what kinds of actions they could do that emulate Jesus' model of service. For example, they could change a little brother or sister's diapers, pick up trash in a park or along a roadside, clean off desks after school, or do laundry for a team after the game. As they call out ideas, make a list on a piece of newsprint or a dry-erase board.

Give each person a small hand towel, a piece of cloth, or a rag. Set out permanent markers or fabric markers.

Say: I'd like each of you to choose one idea you would like to commit to. Write your idea on this towel.

Pause to allow teenagers to write.

Say: Even if you choose not to focus on service as a spiritual discipline, we're required to follow Jesus' example in serving others. I encourage you to follow through on this commitment and take home your towel—a symbol of Jesus' foot-washing service—as a reminder.

Close in prayer, asking for strength, opportunities, and humility to serve.

LEADER TIP

As students leave, remind them to take time this week to read about Mother Teresa in their student journals (p. 30) and record their thoughts and prayers throughout the week.

Try these ideas to incorporate service into your youth ministry program on a regular basis.

● Demonstrate service in your own life. Be an example of humility. Approach youth ministry as serving young people and their families to build their faith, never for your own glory or anything you receive in return.

[BONUS IDEAS

● Organize real service projects for your teenagers: experiences that require true humility and that set up no expectation of glory or anything else in return.

● When teenagers complain about problems they see in the church or the youth ministry, challenge them to solve the problems themselves through service.

● Form a "Service Response Team" of teenagers who are willing to serve in response to needs that arise in your community or elsewhere. Contact local and perhaps national and international relief organizations to let them know that your team is available to help with anything they can when a need arises. Be sure to provide any necessary training. Then when a natural disaster, human tragedy, or other crisis occurs, mobilize your team of volunteers to help however you can!

SERVICE PROJECTS

Photocopy this page, and cut apart the slips of paper. You'll need one slip for each person.

Get someone a glass of water.	Share with someone some encouraging words.	Get someone padding for his or her seat.
Give someone a thirty-second foot massage.	Ask someone what you can pray for, then pray for that person.	Get someone a glass of water.
Get someone padding for his or her seat.	Give someone a thirty-second foot massage.	Don't do anything.
Get someone a glass of water.	Give someone a thirty-second foot massage.	Share with someone some encouraging words.
Share with someone some encouraging words.	Don't do anything.	Ask someone what you can pray for, then pray for that person.
Ask someone what you can pray for, then pray for that person.	Get someone padding for his or her seat.	Don't do anything.

LET'S TALK

PRAYER

In *You Can Make a Difference*, Gary Collins says, "Prayer is not something that occupies an out-of-the-way corner of life. It deals in the realities of daily living...Prayer becomes an ongoing communication between a Christian and the Creator."

Teenagers may feel intimidated by the idea of prayer as a discipline. Rather than thinking of prayer as communication, they may feel like prayer is a performance—a daily requirement for "getting in good" with God. They may fill their prayers with chatter to fulfill the requirement, then move on with life as if the two are disconnected.

Through practicing the spiritual discipline of prayer, teenagers can experience two-way communication with God. Prayer builds faith by helping people know God, hear from God, and express dependence on God.

OPENER

Say: **Let's define communication. Call out words that describe what communication is, and I'll make a list.**

 As young people call out words, write them on a chalkboard or a dry-erase board.

Say: **Now let's work together to use these words to create a definition for communication.**

Lead teenagers in compiling a definition for communication. Write that definition where everyone can see it. Then ask:

- **What elements are required for communication to happen?**
- **What makes for good communication?**

Supplies:

You'll need a chalkboard and chalk or a dry-erase board and a marker, a telephone or a phone receiver, a picture or sculpture of praying hands (draw them yourself if necessary), an invitation, a tool (such as a hammer or a screwdriver), food (such as a slice of bread), Bibles, three dictionaries, newsprint, markers, tape, paper, pens, photocopies of the "Appointment Cards" handout (p. 47), and scissors.

- What destroys communication?
- What role does communication play in relationships? What are some examples of how communication has come into play in your relationships?

Say? Good communication is one of the most important elements of a strong relationship. Today we'll talk about how to communicate with God.

UNDERSTANDING THE DISCIPLINE

Have students form five groups of any size (if necessary, a group can be one person). Give each group one of the following objects: a telephone (or a phone receiver), a picture or sculpture of praying hands (draw them yourself if you need to), an invitation, a tool (such as a hammer or a screwdriver), and food (such as a slice of bread).

Say? As a group, consider how your object symbolizes prayer and what that symbol says about prayer.

After a few minutes of discussion, have each group present its symbol and conclusions regarding prayer. Then ask:
- All put together, what do these symbols teach us about prayer?
- How does prayer help us know God?
- How can we make sure our prayer is effective, two-way communication?
  - How does prayer help us express dependence on God?
  - How can prayer build our relationships with God?

Say? Prayer helps us know God, hear from God, and express dependence on God. God wants all of those things for us. Let's take a look at what God's Word says about God's desire for us.

SCRIPTURE SOURCE

Read Philippians 4:6-7 aloud while students follow along in their Bibles. Then have teenagers form three groups. Give each group a dictionary. If you don't have three dictionaries, just have groups take turns using one. Assign each group one of these words: *petition*, *transcend*, and *anxious*. Give each group a piece of newsprint and a marker.

Say? Look up your assigned word in the dictionary, and write out the definition on newsprint. Be ready to explain the definition to the rest of the group.

When groups have written out their definitions, have each group present its definition and explain it. Then hang the definitions where everyone can see them, and give each group paper and a pen.

Say? Using the definitions we found, work as a group to rewrite Philippians 4:6-7 in your own words.

After a few minutes, have groups present their rewritten versions of the Scripture. Then ask:
- According to these verses, why should we pray?
- How does prayer change us?
- Why would God's peace enter our lives as a result of prayer?
- What do these verses say about prayer and our relationships with God?

Say? Scripture tells us to pray. And it's clear in telling us that prayer will change our lives. Let's practice prayer right now.

PUTTING IT INTO PRACTICE

Have students find their own space in the room and get comfortable.

Say: Feel free to close your eyes and do whatever you need to do to feel comfortable and ready to spend time focused only on God. I'm going to lead you through a series of prayers. I'll give you instructions on the kind of prayer to practice, and you'll have a few moments to do so on your own, either silently or aloud. We'll spend time praising God for who he is and then praising God for what he does, confessing our sins, listening to God, praying for other people's needs, talking to God about our needs and struggles, and thanking God. These are all great ways to pray in your own regular times with God.

First of all, spend a few moments in silent prayer, asking God to make his presence known to you during this time and to help you focus on prayer.

Pause for about thirty seconds to one minute.

Say: Now spend some time praising God for who he is.

Pause for about thirty seconds to one minute.

Say: Now spend some time praising God for the incredible things he does.

Pause for about thirty seconds to one minute.

Say: Now let's confess our sin to God. Talk about the wrong things you've done, and honestly acknowledge your need for God's forgiveness.

Pause for about thirty seconds to one minute.

Say: Next we'll spend a few moments in silence, listening to God. Listen for God to speak to you in silence.

Pause for about thirty seconds to one minute.

Say: Our next time of prayer will be for intercession. Intercession is praying for other people's needs.

Pause for about thirty seconds to one minute.

Say: Now let's present our personal requests to God. This is the time to ask for things you need and to talk to God about struggles you're facing in your life.

Pause for about thirty seconds to one minute.

Say: To close our prayer time, we'll spend a few moments thanking God for listening to us, for providing for us, for loving us, and for everything else God does.

Pause for about thirty seconds to one minute.

Say: Hopefully this time of prayer was meaningful for you. You can incorporate all these types of prayer into your life, whether or not you focus on prayer as a spiritual discipline. Let's consider how we might do that.

CLOSING

Before the lesson, make at least one photocopy of the "Appointment Cards" handout (p. 47). Cut apart the cards. You'll need one card for each person.

Say: In today's hectic world, we often have to set appointments with those we want to spend time with: doctors, teachers, even friends. To spend time in prayer, we may need to make appointments with God so we don't crowd him out of our lives. Let's set appointments with God now.

Give each person a card from the "Appointment Cards" handout and a pen.

Say: Fill in the card with a time and place you will commit to spending time communicating with God through prayer. If you're ready to make a long-term commitment, you may want to set your appointment to happen on an ongoing basis, such as every day or every week.

When students have completed their cards, close with a simple prayer, thanking God for the incredible privilege of communicating with him.

Encourage teenagers to take home their appointment cards and follow through with their commitments. You may want to follow up with them later, just asking whether they've kept their appointments with God.

LEADER TIP

As students leave, remind them to take time this week to read about Martin Luther in their student journals (p. 34) and record their thoughts and prayers throughout the week.

Try these ideas to incorporate prayer into your youth ministry program on a regular basis.

• Use creative methods of prayer with your group. Refer to books on prayer, such as *With Christ in the School of Prayer* by Andrew Murray.

• With your group, periodically watch the evening news or a cable news channel, and pray for the people involved in news stories as they're covered.

[BONUS IDEAS

• Establish a time of day when everyone in your group can spend some time in prayer. The time should be easy to remember, such as noon or the time the school day begins. At that time, everyone in your group should pause to spend some time in prayer in the midst of his or her daily activities.

• Take your group to a mall, an airport, or another crowded public place. Start off with prayer, asking God to open your eyes to the needs of others, to give you compassion for them, and to guide you in your prayers. Then walk through the place, silently praying for those you pass along the way. After the experience, discuss it with your group, talking about how the experience affected them and their faith.

• When teenagers come to you for help or counsel for specific difficulties, include prayer in your helping strategy. Besides praying with the young people, prescribe specific types and amounts of prayer to help them connect with God in the midst of their struggles.

• Focus on prayer by taking your students through *Prayer in Motion* (Group Publishing), a creative four-week course.

APPOINTMENT CARDS

Photocopy and cut apart the cards.

I have an appointment with God:

Date: ....

Time: ....

Place: ....

Some things I want to talk about with God: ....

....

....

....

I have an appointment with God:

Date: ....

Time: ....

Place: ....

Some things I want to talk about with God: ....

....

....

....

WHAT REALLY MATTERS

SCRIPTURE: MARK 8:34-37

SACRIFICE

In his classic devotional *My Utmost for His Highest*, Oswald Chambers said, "God spilt the life of His Son that the world might be saved; are we prepared to spill out our lives for Him?...It is time now to break the life, to cease craving for satisfaction, and to spill the thing out."

Selfishness: It has been a hallmark of humanity since the beginning of time. And teenagers certainly aren't immune. They face the constant temptation to live for themselves, even at the expense of others.

Through practicing the spiritual discipline of sacrifice, teenagers can experience what it's like to live for God rather than for themselves. Sacrifice builds faith by reminding us what we should be living for.

OPENER

Say? I'm going to read some situations aloud. For each one, I'd like you to tell me what the people give up in that situation.

 **A man in a hurry slows down to let someone go ahead of him in the grocery store checkout line.**

Pause and prompt teenagers to tell you what the man gives up.

Say? A high school youth group donates money each month to support a needy child overseas.

Pause and prompt teenagers to tell you what the youth group gives up.

Say? A family donates a used car to a needy family in their church.

Pause and prompt teenagers to tell you what the family gives up.

Say? A child donates some toys to a homeless shelter.

Pause and prompt teenagers to tell you what the child gives up.

Supplies:
You'll need
Bibles,
newsprint, a
marker, index
cards, pens, and
an offering plate
or basket.

Say: A group of college students skips one meal a week and donates the cost of that meal to an organization that helps feed people in need.

Pause and prompt teenagers to tell you what the college students give up.

Say: A frustrated and angry traveler decides to smile at an airline employee instead of complaining.

Pause and prompt teenagers to tell you what the traveler gives up.

Say: A talented teenager postpones art school so he can work to support his mother, who is out of work.

Pause and prompt teenagers to tell you what the teenager gives up.

Ask:

- **What makes something a sacrifice?**
- **What makes a sacrifice worthwhile?**

Say: Jesus asks his followers to live lives of sacrifice. That's always worthwhile. Let's take a look at the discipline of sacrifice.

UNDERSTANDING THE DISCIPLINE

Say: So what does it mean to sacrifice? Sacrificing is giving until it hurts, offering your life as a gift to God. Living a life of sacrifice means your life isn't about you anymore; it's about God.

Ask teenagers to form groups of two to four people. Assign each group one of the following areas: time, money, dreams, appetites, plans, possessions, image, and popularity. It's OK if not all the categories are assigned or if some categories are assigned to more than one group.

Say: I've assigned you some of the different areas of life in which Jesus asks his followers to sacrifice. In your group, come up with a short skit (a minute or shorter) that demonstrates how a

person might give in that area until it hurts, presenting that sacrifice as an offering to God.

Give groups a few minutes to develop their skits, then ask groups to take turns performing their skits for one another. Ask:

- **What are some other ways we might sacrifice as an offering to God?**
- **How might sacrifice affect the way a person experiences God?**
- **Why would sacrifice build a person's relationship with God?**

Say: Let's examine the Scripture source for the discipline of sacrifice.

SCRIPTURE SOURCE

Make sure each person has a Bible. Read Mark 8:34-37 aloud while students follow along in their Bibles. Draw a vertical line down the middle of a piece of newsprint where everyone can see it. Label one column "losses" and the other "gains."

Say: Look at the passage we just read, and notice the losses that are named and the gains that are named. Let's list each.

Ask teenagers to call out losses and gains that are mentioned in the Scripture passage.

Instruct students to look at the list for a moment. Then ask:

- **What do you think these losses and gains represent?**
- **What kinds of things does Jesus ask his followers to sacrifice?**
- **What kinds of things do Jesus' followers gain in return for their sacrifice?**
- **What do these verses say about what we should be living for?**
- **What does a life of this kind of sacrifice look like?**
- **How can sacrifice build our faith in God?**

Say: Sacrifice puts things in perspective. It reminds us what's truly important and what we should be living for. When we give up what's not important in favor of what matters, we're able to see God's truth more clearly. And we experience immense joy in depending on God.

PUTTING IT INTO PRACTICE

Say: Let's spend a few minutes considering what we have that we can sacrifice for God. Think of what you can sacrifice in a way that hurts. If you need ideas, think about the categories we mentioned earlier: time, money, dreams, appetites, plans, posses-sions, image, and popularity. But don't feel you have to limit yourself to those categories.

Give each person an index card and a pen.

Say: On your index card, write a description of something you're willing to sacrifice for God. As a way of showing our commitment to sacrifice, we'll pass around an offering plate and offer these sacrifices to God. If you aren't ready to make a serious commitment to this, don't put your card in the offering.

Pass around an offering plate or basket to collect the cards. Set the offering aside and ask:
- How does it feel to commit yourself to making this sacrifice?
- How will this sacrifice affect your life?
- How might this sacrifice affect your relationship with God?
- Why does God ask us to sacrifice this way?

Say: Remember what's important. You're giving up something with only earthly value so that you can make an investment in God's eternal kingdom. God is pleased with your offering.

CLOSING

Say: In our appetite-driven society, we often complain about what we don't have or can't afford. But God has given each of us an abundance of gifts: time, money, possessions, food, dreams, plans, relationships, knowledge, potential, skills, and others. We can choose how to use these gifts from God. We can choose to throw them away by living selfishly, or we can invest them in things that matter and that will last forever.

Instruct students to close their eyes and get comfortable.

Say: Let's consider honestly before God how we've been using what God has given us. Let's begin in prayer. Dear God, please guide us as we consider our own lives. Help us to be honest with ourselves and you. Holy Spirit, guide us to see our lives clearly.

Pause for a moment.

Say: Silently consider your own life. What kinds of investments have you been making? How do you spend most of your time? Pause for a moment. How do you spend most of your money? Pause for a moment. Do you share your possessions or cling to them for your own pleasure? Pause for a moment. How do you use your food? Pause. your dreams? Pause. your plans? Pause. your relationships? Pause. your knowledge, potential, and skills?

Pause for a moment.

Say: Ask God to show you how you can use those gifts to make investments in the kingdom of heaven—investments in what will last forever.

Pause for several moments.

Say: Thank you, God, for what you've revealed to us. Please change our desires and habits. Inspire us to live lives of sacrifice, just as you made the ultimate sacrifice on our behalf. Amen.

LEADER TIP

As students leave, remind them to take time this week to read about Martin Luther King Jr. in their student journals (p. 38) and record their thoughts and prayers throughout the week.

Try these ideas to incorporate sacrifice into your youth ministry program on a regular basis.

[BONUS IDEAS

• Expose teenagers to the joy of sacrifice by calling them to sacrifice in specific ways, with specific short-term projects that have tangible results. For example, work with Habitat for Humanity to build a house. Go on a short-term missions trip that focuses on helping others. Attend a Group Workcamp to help provide safe and sound homes for people in need. Raise funds for a specific project. Work together to meet a specific need in your church.

• Create a "sacrifice pool." Ask students to name specific sacrifices they're willing to make to meet the needs of others: time, money, possessions, use of specific skills, and so on. Keep a record of these potential sacrifices, and call upon them when they're needed within the church, the youth group, or the community. Make sure you follow through on calling for these sacrifices.

• Challenge your young people to set an example of sacrifice for the rest of the church. For example, teenagers might sacrifice for a specific cause and challenge the rest of the church to match their donations.

Supplies:

You'll need newsprint or a dry-erase board; a marker; packaged foods or personal care products with long, confusing ingredient labels (such as snack cakes and shampoo); Bibles; paper; pens; Bible study tools (such as commentaries, books describing historical context, word-study dictionaries, Bible dictionaries, English-language dictionaries, Bible encyclopedias, concordances, study Bibles, and anything else— maybe even a computer); photocopies of the "Bible Study Bookmarks" handout (p. 56) on card-stock paper; scissors; and markers.

THE MORE TRUTH YOU KNOW...

SCRIPTURE: 2 TIMOTHY 3:14-17

STUDY

In *Experiencing God*, Henry Blackaby says this about studying God's Word: "When you come to understand the spiritual meaning and application of a Scripture passage, God's Spirit has been at work. This does not *lead* you to an encounter with God. That *is* the encounter with God. When God speaks to you through the Bible, He is relating to you in a personal and real way."

Teenagers may feel discouraged and confused when they read the Bible, either not understanding its content or feeling as if the Bible is irrelevant to their lives. Many don't understand that growing from God's Word means more than just reading it. Studying God's Word can reveal the understanding and life-changing truth they need.

Through practicing the spiritual discipline of study, teenagers can understand more about who God is. Study builds faith by bringing people into close encounters with God's powerful truth.

OPENER

Display a piece of newsprint or a dry-erase board.

Say: **Call out some ideas of different study skills and methods people use at school or elsewhere. What are some ways people study?**

As students call out ideas, list them on the newsprint or dry-erase board.

Say: **Today we're going to talk about the spiritual discipline of studying God's Word.**

UNDERSTANDING THE DISCIPLINE

Give students some packaged foods or personal care products with long, confusing ingredient labels.

Say: Pass these products around the group. When a product comes to you, quickly read the ingredient list so you can understand what that product really is.

After students have looked at ingredient labels for a few minutes, ask:

- What did you learn from your reading?
- How did this experience change your life?

Say: Sometimes reading the Bible can feel like reading one of these ingredient labels. The Bible is God's incredible letter to us, and it can change our lives. But if you try to read the Bible and don't understand it, you may become frustrated and quit. Or you may be so confused by what you read that you don't understand how it can change your life. But there's hope! There are many tools available to help us study the Bible, and God's Holy Spirit can guide us as we study.

Ask:
- How can studying help us understand God better?
- How can studying help us spread God's love to others?
- How can studying produce change in our lives?

Say: Let's take a look at what God's Word says about the power of studying the Bible.

SCRIPTURE SOURCE

Read 2 Timothy 3:14-17 aloud. Then have students form groups of three to five, and give each group paper; pens; and a different Bible study tool such as a commentary, a Bible dictionary, a Bible encyclopedia, a concordance, or a study Bible. If possible, assign to each group an adult leader or an older student who can show the group how to use its Bible study tool.

Say: In your group, use the Bible study tool I just gave you to study 2 Timothy 3:14-17. You can study all three verses, just one of the verses, one word, one concept, the history of the time when it was written, or even an overview of the book of 2 Timothy. As you study, prepare a verbal report on what you learn. You'll present that report to the other groups.

 Give groups several minutes to work, warning them when they have only a couple minutes left. Then call time and ask each group to present its report.

Ask:
- What was Paul telling Timothy to do?
- Why did Paul give Timothy this instruction?
- According to these verses, how does God's Word affect us?
- How might studying God's Word affect our relationship with God?
- Why study God's Word?

Say: Studying God's Word teaches us more about who God is. And the more truth we know about God, the more we want to serve God and know him better. Let's practice the discipline of study right now.

PUTTING IT INTO PRACTICE

Ask each student to choose a favorite verse or short Bible passage, or suggest the following ideas: Genesis 11:1-9; Exodus 12:1-30; Psalm 23; Psalm 139; Matthew 5:3-12; Luke 23:26-49; Hebrews 4:12-13; and Hebrews 5:12-14.

Set out Bible study tools such as commentaries, books describing historical and cultural context, word-study dictionaries, Bible dictionaries, regular English-language dictionaries, Bible encyclopedias, concordances, study Bibles, and anything else you can get your hands on (maybe even a computer with a list of suggested, well-respected Bible study Web sites).

Say? **Look up your verse or passage, then use your Bible and these Bible study tools to study your verse or passage. If you find related Bible passages listed in a study Bible or commentary, look those up. Look up key words and concepts and historical and cultural information related to your passage or verse. Do as much as you can to understand the verse or passage. You have fifteen minutes to study.**

Warn students when they have two or three minutes left. After fifteen minutes are up, have them form pairs and tell their partners what they learned.

Ask:

- **What kinds of things did you discover in your study?**
- **How does this affect the way you see this verse or passage?**
- **How can this kind of study help you grow closer to God?**

Say? **Now let's consider how Bible study can become a part of your everyday life.**

CLOSING

Before the lesson, photocopy the "Bible Study Bookmarks" handout (p. 56), preferably on card-stock paper. Cut apart the bookmarks. You'll need one for each person.

Say? **We began this lesson talking about different methods and skills of studying. To close, let's consider what Bible study methods might be effective for us.**

Give each person a bookmark from the "Bible Study Bookmarks" handout. Set out markers and pens.

Say? **On your bookmark, outline at least one study method you think would work well for you in studying the Bible. You may want to personalize and decorate your bookmark too. Refer to the list of study methods we made at the beginning of this lesson if you need ideas. I'll also add some other ideas to the list.**

On the list of study methods created at the beginning of the lesson, add these ideas and any others you come up with: word study (studying the various ways a particular word is used throughout Scripture), studying a particular Bible character or theme, inductive Bible study (observation, interpretation, application), using a devotional, seeking the input of a pastor or someone else trained in theology, and consulting a few different Bible translations to gain new insights.

Give teenagers a few minutes to create their bookmarks. Then encourage them to use the bookmarks in their Bibles.

Say? **Even if you don't choose to intensively focus on the discipline of study at this point, Bible study is an important habit for every Christian to incorporate into life.**

Close in prayer, thanking God for the Bible and asking the Holy Spirit for motivation, encouragement, and guidance in studying God's Word.

LEADER TIP

As students leave, remind them to take time this week to read about John Wesley in their student journals (p. 42) and record their thoughts and prayers throughout the week.

Try these ideas to incorporate study into your youth ministry program on a regular basis.

• Always be responsible in the way you handle Scripture. Using proof-texts, pulling Scripture out of context, and drawing only on Scriptures with "easy" messages are irresponsible ways to present God's Word. In teaching, give students historical, cultural, and literary context. Help them understand where an individual passage fits in the big picture of God's letter to us. Admit that some Scriptures present great mysteries and difficult teachings.

• Challenge students with truths they don't understand. We sell them short if we give them the impression that they've "been there, done that" when it comes to the Bible. Make it clear that in this lifetime we will never "graduate" from Bible study; there are always plenty of new things to learn.

[BONUS IDEAS

• Have teenagers look up Scriptures in their Bibles rather than just listening to them as you read them or reading them from an overhead or program. Get them in the habit of opening their Bibles!

• Incorporate study tools into your teaching. Always have them available. Stop teaching sometimes to have students use them for further understanding on your topic or a Scripture passage. Encourage them to form a habit of stopping you to get clarification any time they don't understand.

• Before Sunday morning services, find out what the text of the message will be. Then encourage students to study the Sunday morning sermon passage ahead of time on their own so that they can get more out of the message. You can also do this the week following the sermon.

BIBLE STUDY BOOKMARKS

Photocopy this page onto card-stock paper, then cut apart the bookmarks.

BIBLE STUDY IDEAS

BIBLE STUDY IDEAS

BIBLE STUDY IDEAS

BIBLE STUDY IDEAS

TRYING TO LAUGH

SCRIPTURE: PSALM 100

CELEBRATION

In his book *The Life You've Always Wanted*, John Ortberg says, "People who want to pursue joy especially need to practice the discipline of celebration. This is a primary reason that we see much emphasis placed on feast days in the Old Testament. Times of feasting were to be transforming experiences—just as times of meditating or fasting were."

Ortberg also says, "Here is a key task for spiritual vitality: *We must arrange life so that sin no longer looks good to us.*"

Teenagers face the same kinds of stresses, boredom, and fears as adults, often before they're ready to handle them. Many approach life with a heavy seriousness that keeps them awake at night; others search desperately for escape from reality. Through the hardships and drudgery of everyday life, it's easy to overlook the amazing gifts of God. And many teenagers aren't quick to see the solution in a relationship with God. If they see church as boring drudgery, they aren't likely to assume Christianity has any sort of solution to the heaviness of life.

Through practicing the spiritual discipline of celebration, teenagers can be reminded of God's great gifts. This lesson can help students really understand what true fun and celebration are! Celebration builds faith by bringing joy and strength as we focus on God's work in the world.

OPENER

Have students form pairs. Instruct partners to try to make each other laugh without touching each other.

Supplies:

You'll need three stacks of paper in three different colors, markers, tape, two kinds of noisemakers, confetti, balloons, streamers and other decorations, snacks, a cassette or CD of upbeat Christian music, a cassette or CD player, construction paper, a three-hole punch, and a three-ring binder.

Say: You have thirty seconds to try to make your partner laugh. Whoever laughs within those thirty seconds is out of the game. Go!

After thirty seconds, call time. Whoever laughed is out of the game. If neither partner laughed, the pair should find new partners. If a person's partner is out, that person should find a new partner. Keep playing the game until only one person is left or until about five minutes have passed.

Ask:

- How easy or hard was this game? Why?
- How did you try to keep from laughing?
- How did you try to make your partner laugh?

Say: This is how some of us live our lives: as if we're trying not to laugh. But instead some of us need to try to laugh! Today we're going to discuss the spiritual discipline of celebration.

UNDERSTANDING THE DISCIPLINE

Before the lesson, set out a stack of paper (all one color), markers, and tape.

Say: Let's think about several bad things that happen in our world; things to be sad about.

Have students write descriptions on the pieces of paper and then tape the papers on the walls of your meeting area. Then instruct teenagers to stand back and look around the room at the messages on the walls.

Ask:

- How does it feel to look around this room?
- How does it feel to think about these things in real life?

Set out a different color of paper.

Say: Now write down descriptions of good things in our world; things to be happy and excited about, gifts from God, things God has done for you specifically, and good things about life.

Have students write their new descriptions and tape the papers on the walls among the papers already there. Then ask them to stand back and look around the room at the messages on the walls.

Ask:

- Now how does it feel to look around this room?
- How does seeing the positive things affect the way you see the negative?
- How do the negatives affect the way you see the positives?
- What might celebrating the positives do to build your faith?

Say: Sometimes we get so focused on the hardships in life that we lose sight of the fact that God is at work in the world. God is always present and shows himself in his creation, our relationships with one another, everyday joys, and miracles. Celebration doesn't mean ignoring the hardships of life; it means affirming and drawing strength from the joys of life and eternity.

Ask:

- How might celebration give us strength to handle the trials in life?
- Why would someone need to practice celebration as a discipline?
- What are some different ways to celebrate?

As teenagers call out answers (such as singing, dancing, laughing, clapping, making music, or shouting), write each one on a third color of paper, and tape each paper to a wall in your meeting area.

Say: Let's explore a Scripture passage about celebration.

SCRIPTURE SOURCE

Have students form five groups of two or more people.

Say: I'm going to assign each group a certain form of celebratory expression. Don't do it yet—I'll tell you when.

Give Group 1 noisemakers, tell Group 2 to clap their hands, give Group 3 a second kind of noisemakers, tell Group 4 to jump around, and give Group 5 confetti.

Say: Let's read Psalm 100 aloud, a verse at a time. Each group will read one verse. After you read your verse, I'd like you to celebrate in the way I've assigned you. Let's read this Scripture in a way that really communicates celebration!

Have students read the psalm a verse at a time, in order. Then, because students may be shy the first time, ask them to read it again—this time celebrating more exuberantly!

Then ask:
- **What was this experience like?**
- **Why was the writer of this psalm celebrating?**
- **How did reading the Scripture this way affect your understanding of it?**
- **How might living in celebration affect our understanding of God?**

Say: Let's experiment with that now by practicing celebration.

PUTTING IT
INTO PRACTICE

Set out noisemakers, confetti, balloons, streamers and other decorations, and snacks. Play some upbeat, celebratory Christian music.

Say: Let's have a party! Let's celebrate God's great gifts to us.

Instruct teenagers to decorate the room and enjoy the snacks you've provided.

Then say: **I'm going to name some categories of life. For each category I name, let's celebrate. Look** around the room at the ways to celebrate that we named earlier. Let's use those celebration ideas. Also, as I name categories, look around at the positive things we thought of to get ideas for specific things to celebrate in each category. Call out those specific ideas as you read or think of them. For example, if I say, "nature," you may look around the room and notice that trees are listed as something to celebrate. You might also see "clapping" listed as a way to celebrate, so you would clap to celebrate God's gift of trees to us.

Name the following categories one at a time. Pause after each one, leading the group in celebrating God's good gifts in that category.
- **relationships**
- **God's provisions**
- **creation**
- **protection**
- **health**
- **miracles**
- **guidance**

Add any other categories that encompass the positive things on the walls.

Say: Wow! God is at work in our world! God's presence is everywhere, and that's reason to celebrate. Celebration can build our faith as it reminds us how wonderful God is and inspires us to trust God more.

CLOSING

Distribute construction paper, and set out markers where everyone can use them.

Say: Let's create a "Book of Celebration" to keep in our meeting area. Each person should create at least one page that celebrates God's goodness in some way. You can create several pages if you'd like to. Remember, you can look around at the walls in this room for ideas.

Give teenagers time to work on their pages, then use a three-hole punch on the papers, and place them in a three-ring binder.

Ask:
- **How can we use this book to celebrate together on an ongoing basis?**
- **What kinds of things might we add to this book over time?**
- **How might this celebration help us grow in our relationships with Christ?**

Encourage teenagers to add to the book over time, even bringing in photos to celebrate God's ongoing goodness in their lives.

Have students form a circle and hold hands. Close in a prayer of celebration, encouraging teenagers to call out things they would like to celebrate.

LEADER TIP

As students leave, remind them to take time this week to read about John Bunyan in their student journals (p. 46) and record their thoughts and prayers throughout the week.

Try these ideas to incorporate celebration into your youth ministry program on a regular basis.

● Create a celebration Web page as a link off your church's site or as its own site. Have students share things with you that they want to celebrate, and add them to the Web site. Encourage teenagers to visit the site frequently to spark celebration.

● Help teenagers sponsor a celebration party for churches in your area. Encourage everyone to come to the party and share rea-

[BONUS IDEAS

sons to celebrate. Provide a party atmosphere and lively worship experiences.

● Institute rite-of-passage celebrations for teenagers when they hit particular milestones: a "This Is Your Life" game for graduation, a devotional book for a thirteenth birthday, bubble gum for getting braces off, a key chain for getting a driver's license.

● In prayer times, ask for celebration requests before prayer requests. Instead of gliding past them in prayer, spend time praising God and expressing joy for each one before moving on to requests.

● Obtain a collection of rhythm instruments such as tambourines, castanets, maracas, claves, and drums. These can enhance your times of singing and even other kinds of celebration.

SUBMISSION

According to Lawrence O. Richards in *The 365-Day Devotional Commentary*, "In Christ submitting isn't an admission of inferiority. It's simply an affirmation that others are valued and important enough to be heard, loved, and their needs responded to. In God's peculiar way it is submission that makes us great."

Teenagers, like the rest of us, experience frustration when they don't get their own way. Rebellion, road rage, violence, and abuse are symptoms of the quest to be number one, no matter who gets in the way. As students of our culture, teenagers are largely unfamiliar with the antidote to frustration: submission.

Through practicing the spiritual discipline of submission, teenagers can experience freedom from frustration. Submission builds faith by helping people give up their ambitions in favor of finding identity and joy in Christ.

Supplies:

You'll need masking tape, Bibles, newsprint or a dry-erase board, a marker, pens, photocopies of the "Identity Contrast" handout (p. 65), an altar of some kind (or materials to create one, such as folding chairs and a tablecloth or a table and candles), a few slips of paper for each person (each about one inch by seven inches), tape, two craft sticks for each person, markers, and a hot-glue gun.

OPENER

Have students form pairs.

Say: I'd like you to talk with your partner about something that frustrates you.

When pairs have had a few minutes to talk, ask volunteers to share what they discussed. Then ask:

- **Why is it so easy to identify our frustrations?**
- **How does frustration affect our lives?**
- **How does frustration affect our spirits?**

Say: The source of many of our frustrations is wanting—and not getting—our own way. Sometimes the cure for frustration is submission. Let's talk about what submission is.

UNDERSTANDING THE DISCIPLINE

Before the lesson, use masking tape to mark an X in the center of your meeting area.

Ask teenagers to form four teams, and send one team to each corner of the room.

Say: **On the count of three, I'd like you to trade corners with another team. There's one catch: To get to your new corner, you have to go across the X in the center of the room.**

Monitor the activity to make sure teenagers don't get too rough as they collide in the center of the room.

Then say: **This activity was a great illustration of what happens when we want our own way and someone else gets in the way of us getting our way. The result is frustration and even hurt. For example, if my brother and I can't agree on what to watch on TV, and my brother wins because he has the remote, I'll probably feel frustrated.**

In contrast, submission is voluntarily giving up your way to let someone else reach his or her goal. Sometimes submission means giving up our own goals to follow God's way instead. Sometimes it means giving up our own way to let someone else have his or her way. For example, if I have the remote, and I choose to watch the show my brother wants to watch, I'm practicing submission. And because I made that choice, I won't be frustrated. Let's trade corners again, this time exhibiting submission to one another.

Encourage students to submit themselves to one another as they carefully trade corners again. Then point out to students that submission doesn't mean letting others force their will upon you and push you aside in an effort to reach the goal. Submission is a choice to voluntarily give up your own goals to let others achieve theirs.

Ask:

- **How did the two corner-trading activities compare?**
- **How do these activities illustrate real-life experiences?**
- **How does submission affect us as a group?**
- **How does submission affect us individually?**
- **How can submission sometimes cure frustration?**
- **What are some situations in which we shouldn't submit to others?**
- **What's the difference between submission and being abused?**

Make clear to teenagers that submission never means doing something wrong or allowing one's self to be abused, bullied, or sexually harassed.

Say: **Submission flows out of the heart. It's not just an action but an attitude and an authentic heart condition. True submission can bring freedom from frustration, setting us free to find our**  **identity and joy in Christ and not in getting our way. Let's explore what the Bible has to say about submission.**

SCRIPTURE SOURCE

Have volunteers read Philippians 2:1-11 aloud a verse at a time. Then display a piece of newsprint or a dry-erase board where everyone can see it. Create a two-column chart with these headings at the top of the two columns: "Who Jesus Is" and "Who Jesus Became."

Say: **Reread Philippians 2:1-11 silently, and look for descriptions of who Jesus is and who Jesus willingly became when he was on earth. Call out items for these two columns as you see them. You can also include descriptions that aren't in this Scripture passage but that you know from other Scripture passages or Bible stories.**

List items on the chart as students call them out. Then ask:

- **What are some of the differences between the two columns?**
- **Why are these differences significant?**
- **What does this chart teach us about Jesus?**
- **Why did Jesus choose this kind of submission?**

Point out that no one made Jesus change in these ways. He chose to submit. Then give each person a pen and a copy of the "Identity Contrast" handout (p. 65).

Say: Now let's consider how we can follow Jesus' example by submitting to God and to others. Complete this handout, considering who you are and who you can become if you practice submission.

After about ten minutes, ask volunteers to share some of their ideas.

Then ask:

- **How might you go about submitting to follow Jesus' example?**
- **How would this kind of change affect your life? others' lives?**
- **How does submission build a person's relationship with God?**

Say: Let's take part in an exercise in submission now.

PUTTING IT INTO PRACTICE

Before the lesson, set up an altar or some kind of special designated space in your room where students can place an offering. For example, you might borrow an altar from your sanctuary, set up two folding chairs side by side with a tablecloth over them, or set up a table with lighted candles.

As you distribute a few slips of paper to each person, say: **Silently consider some sources of frustration in your life. As you think of sources of** frustration, write each one on one of these slips of paper.

When teenagers have had a few minutes to write, say: **Now consider how submission can set you free from some of your frustrations to find joy in Christ. I'd like you to write a "submission solution" on each slip of paper. The solution should be some way you can combat that frustration through submission. The submission can be to God and his will for your life, or it can be to someone else, allowing that person to have his or her way.**

After a few minutes of writing, instruct teenagers to form their paper slips into circles, then link them and tape the ends to make paper chains. Ask students to lay down their chains on the "altar" you created beforehand.

Say: Laying down these chains as an offering to God is a symbol of our submission.

Ask:

- **If you follow through on these submission solutions in your life, how would that change your life?**
- **How would that affect your faith?**
- **How might you follow through?**
- **How can God help you?**

Say: I encourage you to consider submitting in these ways, whether you focus on submission or not.

CLOSING

Give each person two craft sticks. Set out markers and a hot-glue gun. Encourage teenagers to glue their sticks together to form crosses.

Then say: **Come up with a "Submission is like..." comparison that's meaningful to you. For example, you might come up with something such as "Submission is like purposely letting your opponent win a game" or "Submission is like letting** someone else get the credit for your great ideas." As you come up with your comparison, keep in mind the important fact that submission is a choice; it isn't forced upon you.

When students have come up with their comparisons, instruct them to write the comparisons on their crosses.

Say: I encourage you to take your cross home and use it in a way that will remind you of Jesus' ultimate example of submission: becoming human and choosing to die so he could pay for the wrong things we do. Let's follow his example in our own lives.

Close in prayer, asking God to inspire you and your group to submission.

LEADER TIP

As students leave, remind them to take time this week to read about Henri Nouwen in their student journals (p. 50) and record their thoughts and prayers throughout the week.

Try these ideas to incorporate submission into your youth ministry program on a regular basis.

[BONUS IDEAS

• As a church leader, you're in a special position to model submission to teenagers and others in your church and community. Be sure to demonstrate submission in your own relationships at home, at work, and at church. Be sure submission comes through in your actions as well as your words.

• When teenagers complain about your church, your youth ministry, or each other, encourage them to identify the source of their frustration. If the frustration stems from their inability to get what they want, encourage them to practice submission by giving up their own way in favor of someone else's or in deference to God's will.

• Organize an experience for your students that will require them to delve into submission. For example, they could spend a day with developmentally disabled people, elderly people, or children. Require them to allow the people they're spending time with to set the agenda the entire time. Or they might spend the day practicing submission at an amusement park, a mall, or an arcade. Challenge them to find as many ways as possible to put submission into practice—for example, letting everyone else go ahead of them in line.

IDENTITY CONTRAST

In the first column, list characteristics of yourself, including accomplishments and advantages that identify who you are. In the second column, list characteristics of yourself if you choose to practice submission.

Who I Am	Who I Can Become

You'll need a TV,
a CD player and
a CD of
distracting music,
Bibles, *Diving
Deep Student
Journals*, pens or
pencils,
newsprint and
tape or a dry-
erase board, a
marker, earplugs
(optional), paper,
markers,
modeling clay,
small pieces of
fabric, any other
supplies
teenagers might
use to silently
express
themselves to
God, tape or
glue, a piece of
poster board or
heavy paper for
each person, an
on/off switch
(available in
hardware stores)
for each person,
and pens or
markers.

TURNING IT OFF

SCRIPTURE: JAMES 1:19; 1:26; 3:3-8

SILENCE

In his book *The Spirit of the Disciplines*, Dallas Willard says, "In silence we close off our souls from 'sounds,' whether those sounds be noise, music, or words. Total silence is rare, and what we today call 'quiet' usually only amounts to a little less noise. Many people have *never* experienced silence and do *not* even know that they do not know what it is."

Most teenagers, like the rest of us, are addicted to sound. They surround themselves with noise from CD players, televisions, telephones, traffic, friends, and their own chatter. With so many distractions, it's easy to drown out the still, small voice of God and quiet the sounds of spiritual longing in our souls.

Through practicing the spiritual discipline of silence, teenagers can experience deeper, more genuine communion with God. Silence builds faith by helping people become aware of their own spiritual needs and learn to listen to God.

OPENER

Before this lesson, try to make your meeting area as quiet as possible. When everyone has arrived, ask teenagers to sit quietly.

Say: Let's begin.

Don't say anything more. Spend several moments in total silence. Be sure the silence is long enough that people begin to fidget, giggle, or otherwise show discomfort. If students ask why you aren't saying anything, don't respond.

After several moments of uncomfortable silence, ask:

- **How did you feel during our time of silence?**
- **How did you or other people show that you were uncomfortable with the silence?**
- **Why do you think people are so uncomfortable with silence?**
- **Why has silence become so unusual in our world?**

Say: Today we're going to talk about how silence can help us grow in our faith in God.

UNDERSTANDING THE DISCIPLINE

Say: Let's spend a few minutes getting to know each other better. Everyone find a partner. Then sit with your partner so you're facing each other.

When partners are sitting, say: **Now spend a few minutes telling your partner about yourself. Include whatever information you can think to share, such as your full name, what your family is like, where you go to school, what you like to do in your spare time, and your hopes and dreams for the future. We really want to get to know each other as much as we can, and we only have a few minutes, so you and your partner should talk at the same time. Go!**

While students are talking, turn on a TV and a CD player in the room. Run any other appliances you have around, such as a fan or a coffee maker. Then begin speaking or singing loudly. If some teenagers aren't talking, remind them to tell their partners as much information about themselves as they can, talking at the same time as their partners.

After a few moments, begin asking teenagers to help you with various tasks, such as moving the TV to the other side of the room or deciding whether a picture is hanging straight on the wall.

After teenagers have had a few minutes to talk, turn off the appliances, and ask everyone to stop talking. Pause for a moment, then ask:

- **What did you think of this experience?**
- **How well did you get to know your partner?**
- **What might have helped you get to know your partner better than you did?**
- **How did you feel when I turned off everything and everyone stopped talking?**
- **How is this experience similar to our everyday lives?**
- **How is the conversation with your partner similar to the way we interact with God?**

Say: Trying to get to know your partner probably didn't work very well in this experience. When you're trying to get to know someone, it's usually counterproductive to talk and not listen. And the other sounds around you—the TV, the CD player, and me—probably made it difficult to concentrate on even talking to your partner.

This is the way most of us live our lives. We run at least one appliance all the time, and sometimes we use the TV, the CD player, and the telephone all at once. We talk to God sometimes, but we rarely listen to him. And yet we expect to somehow get to know God better.

Ask:

- **How would silence—your own silence and silence in the room around us—have changed this exercise?**
- **How would regular times of silence in your life affect your relationship with God?**
- **What are some of the hindrances to silence in our lives?**
- **What are some ways we could find times of silence in our lives?**

Say: For most of us in today's world, finding total silence is almost impossible, but we can find ways to incorporate some measure of silence into our everyday lives. Let's take a look at what the Bible says about silence.

SCRIPTURE SOURCE

Be sure each person has a Bible and a student journal, and give everyone a pen or pencil.

Say: As we discussed, there are different ways to find times of silence in our lives. One of the most practical ways is to be silent ourselves. The book of James talks about the discipline of not speaking.

On a piece of newsprint or a dry-erase board, write the following Scripture references: James 1:19; James 1:26; and James 3:3-8. Display the newsprint or dry-erase board where everyone can see it.

Say: Let's all read these Scripture passages silently to ourselves. After you've read the verses, spend a few moments in silence, rereading the verses or thinking about what you've read. If you want to, jot down some reflections or questions in your journal.

Allow students a few minutes to read and reflect on the verses, then ask:

- Why do you think James refers to the tongue as such a powerful force?
- How do our words reflect what's in our hearts?
- According to these verses, what are some potential benefits of "taming the tongue"?
- How can practicing silence help us grow in our faith?

Say: I guess we shouldn't be surprised that the discipline of silence doesn't come naturally to us. But because our words are so powerful, we ought to be careful about when we speak and what we say. Taking time to be silent means we can hear God's voice and get to know him better. And as

we grow in our relationships with God, we reflect his character better to people around us.

PUTTING IT INTO PRACTICE

Say: Now let's practice the spiritual discipline of silence by spending some time in as complete a silence as we can achieve. I'd like you to focus on God. We're going to use the spiritual discipline of silence to listen to God, try to get to know him better, and build our faith in him.

As much as possible, eliminate all noise in the meeting area. You may want to distribute earplugs to each person.

Say: Make yourself comfortable, and try to place yourself in a position in which it will be easy to ignore everyone around you. For some of you, this may be your first experience with silence. For others, it may have been the first time you've experienced silence without trying to escape it.

If your mind starts to wander or you become sleepy, change positions or refocus your thoughts on God. Try to do this without talking to God. Just be with God in silence and listen to him. And be sure to keep quiet so others can experience silence. You may want to close your eyes, too, so you can better focus on experiencing silence. As with any discipline, it may be difficult to do this at first, but you can get better at it by practicing over time.

Set out paper, markers, modeling clay, crayons, scissors, glue, small pieces of fabric, tape, foil, chenille wires, paint, paintbrushes, and any other supplies teenagers might use to silently express themselves to God.

Say: During this time of silence, you may want to express yourself to God or express something God is saying to you. Or you may need a way to refocus your thoughts on God. I've set out some supplies to help you do that. Feel free to use anything here, but be sure to do it in a way that maintains the silence in the room and doesn't distract others. And be sure to stay focused on having a quiet spirit and really listening to God.

Allow five to ten minutes of silence, depending on how your students seem to be responding to the opportunity. When time is up, quietly call everyone back together. Ask:

- **What was this experience like?**
- **What made the silence difficult to handle?**
- **How did you feel during that time of silence?**
- **How could regular times of such silence affect your life?**
- **How could times of silence help you grow in your relationship with God?**

Say: **Let's consider how we can create silence in our everyday lives.**

CLOSING

Before this lesson, tape or glue on/off switches to pieces of poster board or heavy paper. Give each person an on/off switch and a pen or marker.

Say: **This on/off switch is a symbol of the opportunity you have to incorporate silence into your life. We all have some noises in our lives that we probably should eliminate altogether, but most of the sounds we experience aren't necessarily bad. In fact, many of them are good, positive** sounds, such as the voices of our parents and friends, beautiful music, and the sounds of people caring for each other.

To practice the discipline of silence, you'll need to spend time tuning out even the good, positive sounds in your life. This on/off switch can remind you of your ability to do that.

Ask:

- **What are some various kinds of noise in our lives?**

Encourage teenagers to call out ideas, then say: **Now think specifically about your own life. If you were to practice the discipline of silence, what are some of the things you could temporarily silence in your life? Think about your own mouth, the voices of your family and friends, the telephone, the TV, your CD player, and so on. Write down your ideas on the paper attached to your on/off switch.**

Give teenagers a few minutes to think and write, then say: **As you consider incorporating the spiritual discipline of silence in your life, refer to this on/off switch. Taking time to "turn off" these sounds could help you grow in your relationship with God, developing a deeper and more authentic faith in Jesus.**

Close in prayer, asking God to create opportunities for silence in the lives of everyone present.

LEADER TIP

As students leave, remind them to take time this week to read about the Trappist monks in their student journals (p. 54) and record their thoughts and prayers throughout the week.

Try these ideas to incorporate silence into your youth ministry program on a regular basis.

[BONUS IDEAS

• Surprise youth with *occasional* silent meetings, spending the entire youth meeting in silence. Especially at first, you may want to plan various silent activities to help teenagers focus their thoughts. Doing this too often will significantly minimize its effect, so be careful. And before going through with a silent meeting, gauge the mood of your students. If they don't seem ready to be silent at that time, go with a back-up plan instead.

• During your singing time, eliminate the singing and the accompaniment. Just display the words where everyone can silently meditate on them.

• Practice the discipline of silence yourself when young people want to talk with you. Be "slow to speak," listening to what they have to say instead.

• Occasionally display slides, pictures, or video footage without sound. This will make a big difference in what young people observe and glean from visual images.

• During youth meetings, sometimes substitute your talk or lesson with a time of silent reflection. Or incorporate a short time of silent prayer into a meeting. This teaches teenagers that corporate prayer doesn't always have to be out loud.

SPIRITUAL
DISCIPLINES
retreat
PLAN

SPIRITUAL
DISCIPLINES
retreat
PLAN

Use this retreat plan to help your students better understand spiritual disciplines and to encourage each person to focus on developing one of the disciplines in his or her life.

SUPPLIES:

You'll need food, games, worship music, musical instruments, and other general retreat supplies. You'll also need the following supplies:

• *Diving Deep Student Journals* (1 for each person)

• 1 roll of adding machine paper

• markers

• tape

• 1 video camera, camera with slide film in it, or digital camera for each team of 6 to 8 people

• boxes, plastic bottles, aluminum cans, or anything else teenagers can write on and stack

• study Bibles

• 1 photocopy of the "Discipline Finder" handout (p. 77) for each person

• pens

• audiocassette prepared beforehand (see "Preparation" section)

• cassette player

• enough photocopies of the "Kingdom Roles" handout (p. 80) so each person will have a tag

• 1 photocopy of the "Kingdom Challenge" handout (p. 81) for each group of 4 or 5

• 1 photocopy of the "Ideas for Practice Session 1" handout (p. 83) for each person

• paper

• earplugs

• 1 photocopy of the "National Identities" handout (p. 85) (more if you have a very large group)

• 4 photocopies of the "Our Lives" handout (p. 86) (more for a very large group)

• 1 photocopy of the "Ideas for Practice Session 2" handout (p. 88) for each person

• commentaries

• information on charitable organizations

• 1 photocopy of the "Preparation Station Instructions" handout (p. 90)

• dirty cloths

• washable markers

• piece of frayed rope

• masking tape

• 1 piece of yarn for each person

• tub

• laundry detergent

• elements for the Lord's Supper

• 1 photocopy of the "Ideas for Practice Session 3" handout (p. 92) for each person

• art supplies

• index cards

• Bible-study resources (such as encyclopedias and dictionaries)

• cleaning supplies

• large cross made from wood or cardboard

• votive candles

• matches

• gift bows

• 1 photocopy of the "Responsive Reading" handout (p. 94) for each person

• projection screen

• VCR or slide projector

• TV or VPU (Video Projection Unit)

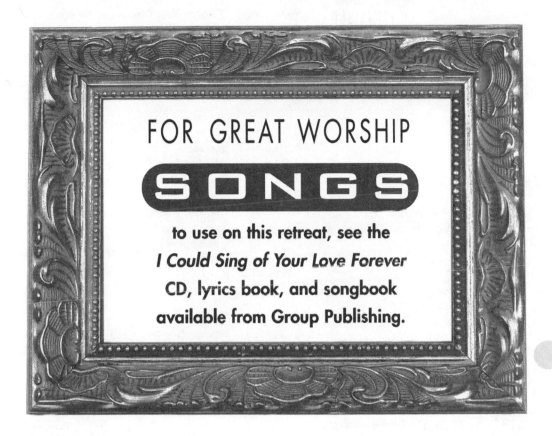

FOR GREAT WORSHIP

SONGS

**to use on this retreat, see the
I Could Sing of Your Love Forever
CD, lyrics book, and songbook
available from Group Publishing.**

PREPARATION

Preparation: Before the retreat, gather all the necessary supplies, and spend some time studying Philippians 3:7-21. Familiarize yourself with the schedule and flow of the retreat. See the suggested schedule on page 74.

Organize the students who will be attending into small groups. If your teenagers already meet in small groups, you may want to consider having them stay in those groups during the retreat. Otherwise, create new groups.

Create an audiocassette of sounds that can inspire worship such as children talking or laughing, water flowing, birds singing, food being eaten, a portion of a positive TV or radio news story, someone saying "I love you," beautiful music, and a dog barking. You'll want at least five minutes of material.

Make photocopies of handouts as listed in the "Supplies" section. Cut apart the tags on the "Kingdom Roles" handout (p. 80). Cut apart the profiles on the "National Identities" handout (p. 85). Cut apart the instructions for the different stations on the "Preparation Station Instructions" handout (p. 90).

suggested retreat SCHEDULE

Friday

7:00 p.m.	arrive at retreat location and settle in
7:30 p.m.	games
8:00 p.m.	Worship Session 1 (see page 74)
8:30 p.m.	Study Session 1 (see page 75)
9:00 p.m.	"Choose Your Discipline" session (see page 76)
10:00 p.m.	Small-Group Session 1 (see page 78)
10:30 p.m.	snacks and free time
12:00 a.m.	lights out

Saturday

8:00 a.m.	breakfast
9:00 a.m.	games
9:30 a.m.	Worship Session 2 (see page 78)
10:00 a.m.	Study Session 2 (see page 78)
10:45 a.m.	Practice Session 1 (see page 82)
11:30 a.m.	Small-Group Session 2 (see page 84)
12:00 p.m.	lunch
1:00 p.m.	free time
5:30 p.m.	dinner
6:30 p.m.	games
7:00 p.m.	Worship Session 3 (see page 84)
7:30 p.m.	Study Session 3 (see page 84)
8:15 p.m.	Practice Session 2 (see page 87)
9:00 p.m.	The Lord's Supper (see page 89)
10:00 p.m.	Small Group Session 3 (see page 91)
10:30 p.m.	snacks and free time
12:00 a.m.	lights out

Sunday

8:00 a.m.	breakfast
9:00 a.m.	Practice Session 3 (see page 92)
10:00 a.m.	"Responding to God" worship service (see page 93)
11:00 a.m.	pack up
11:30 a.m.	depart retreat location

WORSHIP SESSION 1

Open your worship time by singing a few songs. Then remind teenagers that worship is proclaiming the truth, either to ourselves or to others, about who God is and what God does.

Set out a roll of adding machine paper and markers. Encourage young people to unroll the paper and write and draw on it truth about who God is and what God does. Prompt them to use as much of the roll as possible. Remind teenagers to consider this a form of worship. When they've finished, read aloud all or some of the descriptions written on the roll.

Then have teenagers help you decorate the room with the paper, draping it from the ceiling, throwing it over furniture, hanging it like border paper, and so on. When you've decorated the room, worship God together by clapping and cheering for all those great things God is and does.

Have teenagers form teams of six to eight. Give each group a video camera, a camera with slide film in it, or a digital camera.

Say: **We're going to continue worshipping God throughout this retreat. Tonight and tomorrow morning, use this camera to record things to worship God for. We'll use them in our worship later on in the retreat.**

Set a specific time on Saturday for groups to turn in their cameras to you. Once they turn in their work, edit the video footage onto one tape, develop the slides at a one-hour photo shop, or convert

Some photo finishers will develop slides in one or two hours, and some won't. Before you decide to use slides for this worship experience, locate a photo shop near the retreat location that will be open and will develop the slides for you quickly. And be aware that the convenient service will cost you. Be prepared to pay at least ten dollars for one twenty-four exposure roll of slides.

the digital photos into a PowerPoint presentation. You'll need the presentation for Sunday morning.

Close by singing another song if you have time.

STUDY SESSION 1

Scripture: Philippians 3:7-11

Have teenagers form two groups. Give each group markers, and give each person a box. If you don't have boxes, use plastic bottles, cans, or anything else teenagers can write on and stack. Tell one group to write on its boxes things people do that they're ashamed of. Tell the other group to write things people do that they're proud of.

After several minutes, ask the first group to bring its boxes to the front of the room and stack them into a tower while announcing what's written on them. Then ask the second group to bring its boxes to the front of the room and stack them into a tower, announcing what's written on them.

When the towers are stacked, say: **When it comes to being God's child and being accepted by God, these both get you to the same place: nowhere.**

Violently knock down the towers.

Say: **Whether we break God's laws or obey them, whether we make something of our lives or waste them, we can't get God to accept us based on what we do or who we are. Nothing can make us "good enough" for God anyway.**

I'm going to read a Scripture passage, but first I'd like to give you a little background. This passage comes from Philippians 3:7-11. Philippians is a letter that Paul wrote to one of the first churches. Paul was an impressive, respected person. In this letter, he points out some of his credentials. He was part of the tribe of Benjamin, a true Israelite by birth. He was part of a religious group called the Pharisees, who knew Scripture backward and forward. Before he was a Christian, he had been so serious about his beliefs that he had had Christians killed for their beliefs. He had followed God's law faithfully all his life. But listen to what he said about all these credentials.

Read aloud Philippians 3:7-11.

Then ask:

- **What was Paul saying?**
- **What kinds of things was Paul throwing away? Why?**
- **What was Paul looking for in his life?**
- **How did Paul find what he was looking for?**

For game ideas for this retreat, see Group Publishing's great game resources, such as Gigantic Book of Games for Youth Ministry, Volume 1 and Volume 2, On-the-Edge Games for Youth Ministry, and All-Star Games From All-Star Youth Leaders.

Say: Spiritual disciplines don't get us into heaven. They don't even make God love us more. It's very important to understand the purpose of spiritual disciplines: to help us know God better and to help us become more like Jesus. God accepts us as his children when we accept his grace. Spiritual disciplines are a response to that grace.

"Choose Your Discipline" Session

Tell students that this activity will help them consider what spiritual discipline they'd like to focus on during this retreat and perhaps following the retreat. Give everyone a pen and a photocopy of the "Discipline Finder" handout (p. 77).

Give students as much time as they need to complete their handouts. Encourage them to be honest and to pray for wisdom and guidance as the first step. Emphasize that no one but God will see their answers.

Then say: **Take a look at the answers you put on your handout. Did one type of issue come up a lot? If so, I encourage you to focus on that issue in your life right now. If not, pick one issue that you'd really like to work on, and focus on that.** Direct students to the list of disciplines on page 4 of their student journals.

Say: Consider which discipline could help you with the issue you're focusing on. For example, if you feel guilty about not reading the Bible, the discipline of study might be a good one for you to focus on. If you struggle with feeling pressure from the crowd, perhaps you should practice solitude. If you face conflict over little things because you're grouchy, maybe you should try celebration. Mark the discipline you'd like to try.

Give teenagers time to decide which disciplines to focus on. Be available to help students pick which disciplines might work well to address the issues they're facing. Then have everyone find a partner.

Say: Tell your partner which discipline you've decided on. Then tell your partner one idea for incorporating his or her discipline into his or her life. As your partner shares an idea for you, write it in your journal. Then find new partners and repeat. Do this with a total of five partners.

When students have had a chance to share, ask:

- **How can the spiritual discipline you've chosen help address the issue you identified in your life?**
- **How can this spiritual discipline draw you closer to God?**
- **How might this spiritual discipline show your gratitude for God's grace?**

Close by having partners pray for each other.

This retreat works best at a location with plenty of room for teenagers to spread out. It's also best if young people have the option to go outside on their own during portions of the retreat, such as at a retreat center or a camp.

DISCIPLINE FINDER

Pray for God to give you wisdom and boldness to see the truth in your own life. Then honestly answer the questions below, just between you and God.

In your life, what are the areas of greatest spiritual struggle?

What do you often feel guilty about?

What causes a lot of conflict between you and others?

What temptations do you struggle with on an ongoing basis?

How do you feel about your relationship with God?

What do you feel God is telling you right now about the needs in your life?

SMALL-GROUP SESSION 1

Have small-group members introduce themselves to one another.

Then ask:

- **What discipline did you choose? Why?**
- **What do you hope to experience during this retreat?**
- **What are some ways you try to win favor with God?**
- **What's the purpose of practicing spiritual disciplines?**
- **What kinds of things do you think God wants us to avoid when practicing spiritual disciplines?**
- **How can we pray for you?**

Close by praying together.

WORSHIP SESSION 2

Open your worship time by singing a few songs.

Then tell young people that you're going to play a recording of some sounds that can inspire worship. Announce that these sounds represent gifts from God, things in our lives that we should thank and worship God for. Encourage teenagers to respond to God in worship as they listen, praying aloud or silently.

Play the recording you made before the retreat. When the recording is over, encourage teenagers to call out one-word prayers to God, describing other things in life to thank and worship God for.

Close your worship time with as much singing as you have time for.

STUDY SESSION 2

Scripture: Philippians 3:12-16

Announce that you've just been given authority to start a new kingdom. Everyone is in the kingdom, and each person will have a role. Tape a tag from the "Kingdom Roles" handout (p. 80) on each person. It's OK if specific roles are given to more than one person.

When everyone has a role, have students form groups of four or five. Give each group a photocopy of the "Kingdom Challenge" handout (p. 81). Tell students that the handout describes some challenges your kingdom is facing already. Challenge people to think with the identities they've been assigned. Groups should work for ten minutes to come up with solutions to the challenges. After ten minutes, have groups share the solutions they came up with.

Ask:

- **What made this activity easy?**
- **What made this activity difficult?**
- **What are some specific ways you lived out your roles?**

Say: Just as you had to live up to the identity I gave you, we're called to live up to the identity God gives us. God calls us his children.

Read aloud Philippians 3:12-16.

Ask:

- **What did Paul say about perfection?**
- **What was Paul's strategy for spiritual growth?**
- **What does "let us live up to what we have already attained" mean?**

Say: Jesus died in our place to pay for our sins. If we accept that payment for our sins, God forgives us for all those wrong things we've done. He gives us the wonderful identity of being his own forgiven children, as if we are perfect and we have never done anything wrong. Do spiritual disciplines help us get to that position? No, we can't earn it. But we can try to live up to it.

Ask:

- **If we can't be perfect on our own, why try to live up to that identity?**
- **How can spiritual disciplines help us live up to it?**

- What would motivate us to be spiritually disciplined?

Say: Next we're going to practice our chosen disciplines. As you do so, keep your motivation in mind. Instead of trying to earn God's favor, do this as a way to live up to the identity God has given you.

KINGDOM ROLES

Photocopy this page, and cut apart the roles below. You'll need one role for each person.

Prince	Cook
Princess	Director of Fashion
Peasant	Jester
Farmer	Duke of Entertainment
Minister of Finance	Earl of Relaxation
Chief Cook	Prince
Cook	Royal Bowling Instructor
Jester	Cook
Secretary of Education	Princess
Peasant	Peasant
Royal DJ	Farmer
Farmer	Youth Director

KINGDOM CHALLENGE

With your group, come up with solutions to the challenges below.

CHALLENGE 1

The kingdom is facing a budget crunch. Something has to give. We can cut education, defense, entertainment, the arts, or farmers' subsidies.

CHALLENGE 2

The gardener was fired, and someone has to take over the duties, single-handedly maintaining 10,000 acres of land. Who will it be?

CHALLENGE 3

The king is building a new castle. So far, the castle has twenty-two bedrooms, a bathroom, a kitchen, a coat closet, a living room, a dining room, and a room for his baseball card collection. There are 10,000 more square feet of unplanned space. The king wants input on how to use and decorate the 10,000 square feet.

PRACTICE SESSION 1

Tell students that they're going to spend some time practicing their chosen disciplines. Give each person a photocopy of the "Ideas for Practice Session 1" handout (p. 83). Have students turn to the list of spiritual disciplines on page 4 in their student journals.

Tell students that the handout will give them an idea for practicing each discipline on the list in their journals. If they have different ideas for how to practice their chosen disciplines, assure them that that's fine as long as they really are ways of practicing the disciplines and will draw them closer to God.

Tell students that they have about thirty minutes to practice and then they'll spend some time in small groups. Encourage them to use all the time to practice spiritual discipline. And remind them that these practice sessions aren't the only times for them to practice discipline throughout the retreat.

Make sure everyone has the supplies he or she needs (some students may need study Bibles, paper, pens, or earplugs). Allow teenagers to spread out throughout your retreat location (including outside and in other buildings). Provide parameters if certain areas are off limits. As they practice, walk around the area, along with other adult leaders, to help keep everyone on task. When time is up, gather the students into their small groups.

IDEAS FOR PRACTICE
SESSION 1

Worship—Walk around the retreat location, and let everything you encounter remind you of truth about God. Proclaim that truth to God.

Solitude—Be alone with God. Write in your journal your thoughts and what you hear from God.

Fellowship—In your journal, write a letter to someone you want to have fellowship with. Tell that person how you want to fellowship.

Confession—Tell God aloud about sins you've committed in the past.

Fasting—Begin your fast now, and continue it all day or all retreat. Spend time thinking about God and praying. When you think about the item you're fasting from, let that remind you to turn your focus toward God.

Silence—Spend time in silence. Don't talk or write anything. Just listen and focus on God. Wear earplugs if necessary.

Prayer—Pray aloud about everything you can think of.

Sacrifice—Change living arrangements by giving away your pillow, putting yourself in the least desirable sleeping spot, signing up for the least popular free-time activities, putting yourself at the end of the shower sign-up, deciding to sit where no one else wants to sit at meals and sessions, and anything else you can think of. Do this all for the benefit of others.

Study—Pick a passage of Scripture, and read the notes in a study Bible. Write down your insights in your journal.

Celebration—Enjoy a gift God has given you—something you brought with you. Perhaps it's something you've taken for granted (like your toothbrush). Thank God for it.

Submission—List everything good you want to happen to you at the retreat, then give each item to God. Refuse to try to make any of these things happen. Instead, allow God to take over the retreat.

Service—Find a person who volunteered to help make this retreat possible, such as someone working in the kitchen. Help that person, or take over the person's work.

SMALL-GROUP SESSION 2

Have small-group members remind one another of their names and who has what discipline.

Then ask:

- **What did you experience in practicing discipline today?**
- **How has your discipline affected your relationship with God?**
- **What's your motivation for practicing spiritual discipline?**
- **How can your discipline help you live up to your identity in Christ?**
- **How can your discipline help you express gratitude to God?**
- **How can we pray for you?**

Close by praying together.

WORSHIP SESSION 3

For this worship session, simply spend time in singing and prayer.

STUDY SESSION 3

Scripture: Philippians 3:17-21

Have students form four groups. Give each group one of the profiles from the "National Identities" handout (p. 85). If you have a very large group, form more than four groups, and assign some or all profiles to more than one group.

 Also give each group a pen and a photocopy of the "Our Lives" handout (p. 86).

Instruct groups to read their profiles and fill out their "Our Lives" handouts from the perspectives of the people described in their profiles.

When groups have finished working, have them present the answers on their "Our Lives" handouts to everyone else.

Ask:

- **How did your nationality affect your perspective on life?**
- **Why did your nationality affect your answers to the questions?**

Say Paul had something to say about our *spiritual* nationality.

Read aloud Philippians 3:17-21 while teenagers follow along.

Ask:

- **According to Paul, what's our spiritual nationality?**
- **How should our citizenship in heaven affect the way we live?**
- **As Christians, how should we be different from others?**
- **How can spiritual disciplines help us have the right perspective?**

Say We're called to live as citizens of heaven, thinking of eternity and focusing on being with God. Spiritual disciplines help us do that by renewing our perspective. As you practice spiritual discipline, keep your eyes on Christ. Look forward to the day he'll transform us.

NATIONAL IDENTITIES

Photocopy this page, and cut apart the four identity descriptions below.

APADLING SOCIETY

Your society is peaceful. In fact, you really don't like conflict. If Apadlings get in an argument or a fight, they're immediately banished, and the government won't let them back in until they make up. You believe the greatest good is peace and harmony, and you strive for a day when people will live in agreement. Your national symbol is the zucchini, which you harvest. You consider zucchini to be a peaceful vegetable. You use zucchini for trade and currency.

TEANO SOCIETY

Your society is artistic. Everything in your country must be beautiful and highly decorated. You sometimes get used to decorations so that they don't seem like decorations anymore and you have to add more. Everyone got used to the statue in the capitol courtyard, so you planted ivy to grow over it. Then everyone got used to that, so you hung bulbs on it. Then everyone got used to that, so you decorated it with rhinestones. Teanos are always creating artistic masterpieces; they never rest. You dream of the day when the decorating will be finished and you can rest and relax forever. Your national symbol is the paintbrush.

FERLUX SOCIETY

Your society is suspicious of outsiders. You've heard horror stories of what happens when countries are invaded by other nationalities, and you don't want it to happen to you. You spent fourteen years building a wall that surrounds your country. You believe the wall has kept people out of your country. And it also keeps people in. You'd prefer to just forget that anyone else exists. Children are taught that no one lives outside the wall. Your national symbol is the skunk because it manages to keep people away.

GLADGER SOCIETY

Your society is efficient. You don't waste effort, words, time, tools, food, belongings, fabric, or energy. You speak quickly so you can move on to the next activity. If people get in your way, you run them over if you have to—no stopping. If people lag behind, they're thrown out of the country. Inefficiency is unacceptable for a Gladger. You all look forward to the day when your society will run so smoothly that no one will have to think or feel a thing! Your national symbol is a can of oil because you consider yourselves a well-oiled machine.

 **LIVES**

Fill in each of the items below, from the perspective of the national identity your group has been assigned. Be creative!

What gives us hope:...

Our favorite things to do:...

Our purpose in life:..

What makes us sad:...

What makes us happy:...

Our greatest heroes:...

What we're really proud of:..

PRACTICE SESSION 2

Tell students that it's time for another session of practicing spiritual discipline. Give each person a photocopy of the "Ideas for Practice Session 2" handout (p. 88). Have students turn to the list of spiritual disciplines on page 4 in their student journals.

Tell students that they have about thirty minutes to practice and then they'll participate in the

Lord's Supper together. Make sure everyone has the supplies he or she needs (some students may need study Bibles, commentaries, paper, pens, materials to prepare snacks for this evening, earplugs, or information on charitable organizations).

You may want to use this time to set up for the Lord's Supper (see instructions on page 89). When time is up, gather everyone for a celebration of the Lord's Supper.

Worship—In your journal, write descriptive words to praise God.

Solitude—Be alone with God, talking aloud to God and pausing to listen.

Fellowship—If others have chosen to focus on fellowship, fellowship with them. If not, plan a fellowship event that you'll host for other people later on.

Confession—In your journal, write about ongoing sins in your life and sins you've committed this week.

Fasting—Talk to God about how fasting is helping you experience him.

Silence—Walk around the retreat area with earplugs in. Talk silently to God about everything you notice.

Prayer—In your journal, write prayers to God.

Sacrifice—If others have chosen sacrifice, get together with those people. If not, do this alone. Look through information on charitable organizations, and pick one to support financially or through volunteer efforts. Come up with a plan to do this in a way that will be a sacrifice for you. Write your plan in your journal.

Study—Pick a passage of Scripture, and consult a commentary and a study Bible to get more information on it. Write down your insights in your journal.

Celebration—Express joy in God in as many ways as you can come up with. Laugh, smile, jump up and down, whatever!

Submission—Think about areas of life in which you experience frustration and/or worry. One at a time, commit those areas of life to God, giving up your desires in those areas. Submit to God.

Service—Prepare some good snacks for everyone (except those who may be fasting) to eat tonight.

The Lord's Supper

Before this session, set up five stations in your meeting area. Try to make the environment as worshipful and reflective as possible, perhaps with dim light and lighted candles in the room. Place the following supplies at each station:

Station 1—Place the "Instructions for Station 1" from the "Preparation Station Instructions" handout (p. 90). Station an adult leader here (an accepting person your teenagers trust; a good listener). This adult leader should invite teenagers to confess sin to him or her if they want to talk to someone in addition to God. Also place dirty cloths and washable markers at this station.

Station 2—Place the "Instructions for Station 2" from the "Preparation Station Instructions" handout (p. 90). Also set out a piece of frayed rope, masking tape, a marker, and a piece of yarn for each person.

Station 3—Place the "Instructions for Station 3" from the "Preparation Station Instructions" handout (p. 90). Also set out a tub with hot water and laundry detergent in it.

Station 4—Place the "Instructions for Station 4" from the "Preparation Station Instructions" handout (p. 90). Also set out sample elements for the Lord's Supper and at least one Bible, open to 1 Corinthians 11:23-26. Label the bread with a sign saying, "This represents Jesus' body, which was broken in death for you." Label the drink with a sign saying, "This represents Jesus' blood, which was spilled out to pay for your sins so you can have a relationship with God."

Station 5—Set out elements for the Lord's Supper. This is where you'll serve the Lord's Supper to teenagers.

When young people have gathered, point out the five stations you set up beforehand. Tell them that they're now going to participate in the Lord's Supper together. Remind them that this worship experience commemorates Jesus' sacrifice on our behalf and symbolizes our acceptance of Jesus' payment for our sins. Tell them that before participating in the Lord's Supper, they'll go through a series of experiences to prepare.

Say? The Lord's Supper shouldn't be taken lightly. This is a serious act of worship and commitment. After going through these preparation experiences, some of you may feel that you aren't ready to participate seriously in that act. For example, maybe you aren't ready to make a relationship right, you haven't accepted God's forgiveness, you're refusing to confess sin, or you don't understand what all this means. That's OK. Just quietly sit off to the side and spend some time with God as others are worshipping.

Ask a few students to go to Station 1 and follow the instructions. When at least a couple of them have moved on to Station 2, allow a few more students to begin. Continue to stagger groups until everyone has begun the experience.

When students arrive at Station 5, serve the Lord's Supper. Then ask them to sit quietly off to the side, praying and allowing others to have meaningful experiences with God. If a few students are still participating when it's time for small groups, allow those who have finished to go to small groups.

PREPARATION STATION

INSTRUCTIONS

Photocopy this page, and cut apart the sets of instructions. Place the instructions at the stations for the Lord's Supper preparation experience.

INSTRUCTIONS FOR STATION 1—CONFESSION

Spend some time in prayer, confessing honestly to God the wrong you've done. Be open with God about the sin in your life—both actions and attitudes. If you want to continue the confession experience, talk to the adult leader about the sin in your life. Then take one of the cloths. Use a marker to write on that cloth about sins you've confessed to God. When you've finished, go to Station 2, carrying your cloth with you.

INSTRUCTIONS FOR STATION 2—RECONCILIATION

Look at the piece of frayed rope. Consider the rope as a representation of your social life. Each strand represents a person whose life is intertwined with yours. Each strand may be a friend, an acquaintance, or someone you don't like. Think about these questions:
- **What do those frayed ends represent?**
- **What relationships in your life need mending?**

If you need to mend a relationship with a person who is here, go make things right now. If you need to mend relationships with people who aren't here, write each person's name on a piece of masking tape. Put those pieces of tape on a piece of yarn as a commitment to make things right with those people. Then go to Station 3, carrying the yarn with you.

INSTRUCTIONS FOR STATION 3—FORGIVENESS

Pray your repentance, telling God you're sorry for the wrong things you've done. Ask for God's forgiveness. Then experience a symbol of God's forgiveness by throwing your cloth into the tub of water to get clean. Then go to Station 4.

INSTRUCTIONS FOR STATION 4—PREPARATION

In the open Bible, read about the Lord's Supper in 1 Corinthians 11:23-26. Then read the labels on the bread and the drink. Spend some time thinking about those descriptions and praying for understanding. Ask God to make you ready to participate in the Lord's Supper. Then move on to Station 5.

SMALL-GROUP SESSION 3

Ask each small-group member to talk about the best thing that has happened so far on this retreat.

Then ask:

- **What did you experience in practicing discipline today?**
- **How has your discipline affected your relationship with God?**
- **What do the words "you're a citizen of heaven" mean to you?**
- **How should that citizenship affect your life?**
- **How can your discipline help you express your "spiritual citizenship"?**
- **How can we pray for you?**

Close by praying together.

PRACTICE SESSION 3

Give each person a photocopy of the "Ideas for Practice Session 3" handout (p. 92). Have students turn to the list of spiritual disciplines on page 92 in their student journals.

 Tell students that they have about forty-five minutes to practice and then they'll participate in a worship service together. Make sure everyone has the supplies they need (some students may need art supplies; index cards; study Bibles; Bible study resources such as encyclopedias, dictionaries, or commentaries; paper, pens, cleaning supplies; or earplugs). When time is up, gather everyone for a worship service.

IDEAS FOR PRACTICE
SESSION 3

Worship—Tell God the story of your life, highlighting all the ways you've noticed his presence in that story.

Solitude—Spend time alone with God, using your body to express what you're feeling, such as by kneeling before God, bowing down to God, holding your hands up, or looking up.

Fellowship—If others chose fellowship, fellowship with them. If not, think of other Christians in your life, and put each name on a separate index card. Then on each card, write ideas for fellowship with that person. Later on, put these cards together in a card file to follow through on.

Confession—Silently confess sin patterns in your life, including sins that you anticipate you'll continue to struggle with in the future.

Fasting—In your journal, list ways to focus on God while fasting.

Silence—Spend time in silence (using earplugs if necessary), listening to God. Respond to God physically (kneeling before God, bowing down to God, raising your hands, and so on), but don't make any sound.

Prayer—As a way to stay focused on prayer, pray silently though the alphabet, talking with God about something for each letter.

Sacrifice—Give away or get rid of something valuable or meaningful that you brought with you.

Study—Pick a Scripture passage, and read it in a study Bible. Then consult a resource such as an encyclopedia, dictionary, or commentary. Write down your insights in your journal.

Celebration—In your journal, make a list or create artwork that symbolizes gifts God has given you. Include things you can celebrate now and later, after the retreat. Thank God for them.

Submission—Think of frustrations in your life, and write a description of each one on a separate index card. Then on each card, write ideas for submission to address that frustration. Later, put these cards together in a card file to follow through on.

Service—Clean the sleeping quarters and bathrooms (as much as you can get done in the time available).

"Responding to God" Worship Service

Scripture: Philippians 3:7-21

Before this worship service, you may want to talk to a couple of students who are willing to start off the time of sharing about their experiences during the retreat. Lay a large cross (made of wood or cardboard) on the floor in the middle of the room. Set out votive candles, matches, and gift bows next to the cross.

Give each person a photocopy of the "Responsive Reading" handout (p. 94). Have teenagers form three groups.

Say: **Let's read together the passage of Scripture we've covered on this retreat. We'll do this in a creative way, breaking up the passage into short segments and having each group read some of those segments. Remember, this is a worship experience, a reading of God's holy Scripture. As we read, try to focus on the words and read with expression.**

Read the "Worship Leader" parts as you do the responsive reading of Philippians 3:7-21 on page 94 together. Then have teenagers gather around the cross, candles, matches, and gift bows you set out beforehand.

Say: **This cross represents the intervention of God's grace in our lives. Let's respond to that gift now by sharing what we've experienced on this retreat and what we've resolved to do when we go home. As you share an experience you had with God this weekend, light a candle and place it on the cross. As you share a resolution for after you go home, place a gift bow on the cross. The candles represent the moments of light that God brings into our lives. The bows represent gifts we offer God in return, to live up to what God has given us.**

Allow as much time as possible for students to share, and be sure that you share also.

 After everyone has had a chance to share, play the video or slides that students created during the retreat. Remind students to have fun seeing their work but also to use this as a guide for worship. Encourage them to proclaim truth about God as they're reminded of that truth through the video or slides.

Use the remaining time to sing and pray in response to God.

RESPONSIVE READING

PHILIPPIANS 3:7-21

Worship Leader: But whatever was to my profit I now consider loss for the sake of Christ.

Group 1: What is more, I consider everything a loss compared to the surpassing greatness of knowing Christ Jesus my Lord,

Group 2: for whose sake I have lost all things.

Group 3: I consider them rubbish, that I may gain Christ

Group 1: and be found in him,

Group 2: not having a righteousness of my own that comes from the law,

Group 3: but that which is through faith in Christ—the righteousness that comes from God and is by faith.

Worship Leader: I want to know Christ and the power of his resurrection and the fellowship of sharing in his sufferings, becoming like him in his death, and so, somehow, to attain to the resurrection from the dead.

Group 1: Not that I have already obtained all this,

Group 2: or have already been made perfect,

Group 3: but I press on to take hold of that for which Christ Jesus took hold of me.

Worship Leader: Brothers, I do not consider myself yet to have taken hold of it.

Group 1: But one thing I do:

Group 2: Forgetting what is behind and straining toward what is ahead,

Group 3: I press on toward the goal to win the prize for which God has called me heavenward in Christ Jesus.

Worship Leader: All of us who are mature should take such a view of things.

Group 1: And if on some point you think differently,

Group 2: that too God will make clear to you.

Group 3: Only let us live up to what we have already attained.

Worship Leader: Join with others in following my example, brothers, and take note of those who live according to the pattern we gave you.

Group 1: For, as I have often told you before and now say again even with tears, many live as enemies of the cross of Christ.

Group 2: Their destiny is destruction,

Group 3: their god is their stomach,

Group 1: and their glory is in their shame.

Group 2: Their mind is on earthly things.

Group 3: But our citizenship is in heaven.

All: And we eagerly await a Savior from there, the Lord Jesus Christ, who, by the power that enables him to bring everything under his control, will transform our lowly bodies so that they will be like his glorious body.

SCRIPTURE INDEX

Psalm 100 . . . . 57, 59

Psalm 103 14

Mark 1:35-39 . . . . 18, 19

Mark 6:45-51 . . . . 18, 19

Mark 8:34-37 . . . . 48, 49

Mark 9:33-35 . . . . 37, 38

Mark 14:32-43 . . . . 18, 19

John 6:35 . . . . 33, 34

John 13:1-15 . . . . 37, 39

1 Corinthians 9:24-27 . . . . 8, 9

1 Corinthians 11:23-26 . . . . 89, 90

Ephesians 4:11-16 . . . . 23, 25

Philippians 2:1-11 . . . . 61, 22

Philippians 3:7-11 75

Philippians 3:7-21 . . . . 73, 93, 94

Philippians 3:12-16 78

Philippians 3:17-21 84

Philippians 4:6-7 . . . . 43, 44

2 Timothy 3:14-17 . . . . 52, 53

James 1:19 . . . . 66, 68

James 1:26 . . . . 66, 68

James 3:3-8 . . . . 66, 68

James 5:13-16 . . . . 29, 30

1 John 1:8-10 . . . . 29, 30

Group Publishing, Inc. • Attention: Product Development
P.O. Box 481 • Loveland, CO 80539
Fax: (970) 679-4370

Evaluation for *Diving Deep: Experiencing Jesus Through Spiritual Disciplines*

Please help Group Publishing, Inc. continue to provide innovative and useful resources for ministry. Please take a moment to fill out this evaluation and mail or fax it to us. Thanks!

● ● ●

1. As a whole, this book has been (circle one)

not very helpful   very helpful

1   2   3   4   5   6   7   8   9   10

2. The best things about this book:

3. Ways this book could be improved:

4. Things I will change because of this book:

5. Other books I'd like to see Group publish in the future:

6. Would you be interested in field-testing future Group products and giving us your feedback? If so, please fill in the information below:

Name_____

Church Name _____

Denomination _____ Church Size _____

Church Address _____

City _____ State _____ ZIP _____

Church Phone _____

E-mail _____